ADVENTURE TREKS
NEPAL

Bill O'Connor

The Crowood Press

First published in 1990 by
The Crowood Press
Ramsbury, Marlborough
Wiltshire SN8 2HE

British Library Cataloguing in Publication Data

O'Connor, Bill
  Adventure treks: Nepal.
  1. Nepal. Visitors' guides
  I. Title
  915.49'604

ISBN 1 85223 306 0

Series editor John Cleare

All colour photographs by the author except where stated
otherwise; all maps by Don Sargeant.

Typeset by Action Typesetting Limited, Gloucester
Printed and bound in Spain by
Graficas Estella, S.A. (Navarra)

Dedication

*Tread softly, for this is holy
    ground.
It may be, could we look with
    seeing eyes,
This spot we stand upon is
    paradise.*

Christina Rossetti

For my sons, James, Duncan and William;
their journey just begun . . .

Contents

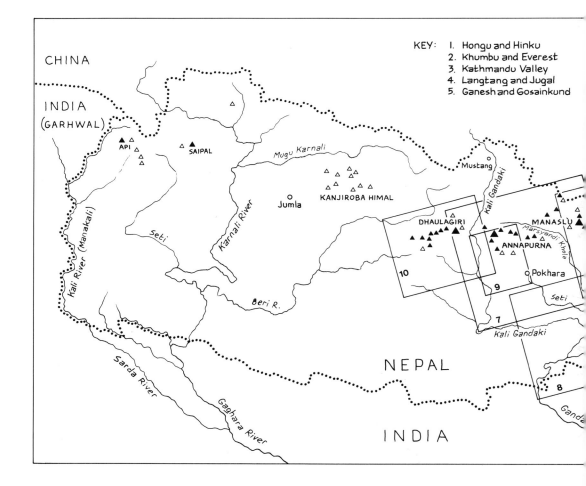

KEY: 1. Hongu and Hinku
2. Khumbu and Everest
3. Kathmandu Valley
4. Langtang and Jugal
5. Ganesh and Gosainkund

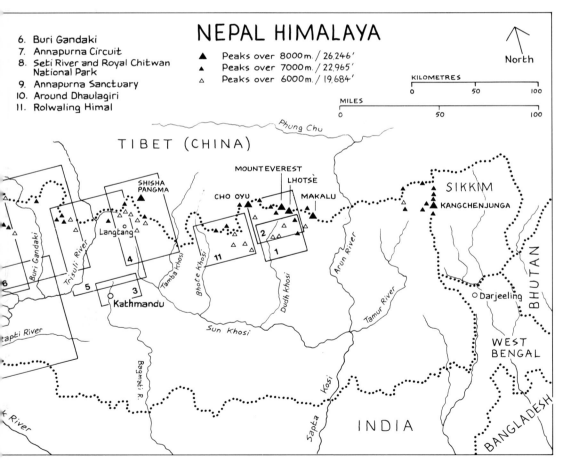

NEPAL HIMALAYA

6. Buri Gandaki
7. Annapurna Circuit
8. Seti River and Royal Chitwan National Park
9. Annapurna Sanctuary
10. Around Dhaulagiri
11. Rolwaling Himal

▲ Peaks over 8000 m. / 26,246'
▲ Peaks over 7000 m. / 22,965'
△ Peaks over 6000 m. / 19,684'

North

KILOMETRES
0   50   100

MILES
0   50   100

TIBET (CHINA)

Phung Chu

SHISHA PANGMA

MOUNT EVEREST

LHOTSE

CHO OYU

MAKALU

SIKKIM

KANGCHENJUNGA

Langtang

Buri Gandaki

Trisuli River

Tamba Khosi

Bhote Khosi

Dudh Khosi

Arun River

Tamur River

Darjeeling

BHUTAN

Kathmandu

Sun Khosi

Bagmati R.

Kosi

Sapta Kosi

apti River

k River

INDIA

WEST BENGAL

BANGLADESH

Preface

'Travel,' wrote Francis Bacon nearly four hundred years ago, 'is a part of education.' It is indeed, but it is also far more than that. Many — and not only altruistic dreamers — see the burgeoning travels of today's common man as an important key to international understanding and future world harmony. Others — more pessimistic yet perhaps more perceptive — see the profligate scatter of the tourist dollar as enriching local economies while despoiling subtle cultures and eroding fragile environments, a typical scenario in the Third World. There is much truth in both views. Travel is surely a two-edged sword.

Thus we who travel and enjoy the wild places — at risk by their very definition — bear a heavy responsibility. It is up to us to do the right thing, to set the right example, and back at home thoughtfully to champion the cause of the wilderness. It is all too easy to kill the goose that lays the golden eggs. The closure of the exquisite Nanda Devi Sanctuary by the Indian Government in 1983 is a case in point where excessive use, abandoned rubbish and environmental pollution had jeopardized its very essence. And, in the scope of this present book, the area of Everest Base Camp could so easily go the same way. Not only must the dictum *Leave nothing but footprints take nothing but photographs* be scrupulously observed but, although this may sound patronising, relations with unsophisticated (to our way of thinking) local people should be tempered with understanding and due consideration. Instant but ill-conceived charity may well spell long-term misfortune for the recipient, as the author will explain. There is no way the world can be understood without seeing it for oneself.

This book is one of the first of our on-going series of ADVENTURE TREKS titles, which set out to encourage the discerning traveller to undertake and enjoy journeys on foot — treks, hikes, walks, call them what you will — through many of the best locations for such activities among the world's wild places. The series covers regions of both the First, Second and Third Worlds (so called), typically in mountain or upland country because that is where the most interesting routes are usually found, with difficulties and commitments to suit most tastes, and always mindful of the considerations discussed above.

Most travel books fall into one of two categories. Some are guidebooks pure and simple, usually useful and at best even interesting, if hardly a 'good read'. Others are narrative accounts, readable, fascinating, often extremely entertaining, but typically ignoring disdainfully any desire of readers to repeat the journey themselves. Hopefully the 'Adventure Treks' series embraces something of both, being entertaining and enthusing — albeit itchy-footedly — while pointing the traveller on his way with first-hand practical advice and crucial information.

Bill O'Connor, the author of this volume, is a sensitive man and as excellent a travelling companion as one could find. He knows Nepal and its people well and has carefully selected ten itineraries which visit many of the most beautiful regions in a charming country. Take his advice and you will enjoy Nepal.

John Cleare

Introduction

I well remember the celebrations at home and at school in 1953, when, with impeccable timing, John Hunt's team reached the summit of Everest in time for the Coronation. It seemed an auspicious start to a new Elizabethan age. I had no idea where Everest was, but in my ancient school atlas it appeared to be part of British India — faded pink and a remnant of Empire. To a schoolboy hooked on exploration, Tensing and Hillary became new heroes, replacing Shackleton (now reinstated) as the one in whose footsteps I wanted to tread.

Not surprisingly, Nepal was then an unknown quantity to me, as indeed it was to most other people. For this tiny land-locked kingdom of 147,181 square kilometres (56,831 square miles), literally concertinaed between the masses of India and the now Chinese-occupied Tibet, had only opened its borders to Western explorers in 1949. That is not to say, as Bill Tilman pointed out 'that Nepal was *terra incognita* — but it is true to say that it was the largest inhabited country still unexplored by Europeans'.

Nepal has had a turbulent history of internal strife, resulting in the xenophobic reaction of its rulers to the 'foreign devil', already so close to its borders where the 'Great Game' was being played. Indeed, during the 'Race to Lhasa' pundits like Hari Ram, in the service of Empire, traversed Nepal incognito dressed as pilgrims *en route* to Tibet, to carry out painstaking surveys. The pundits were preceded by Johann Greber and Albert d'Orville, Jesuit missionaries who passed from Tibet via Tingri down the Bhote Khosi to Kathmandu before returning to Rome. Since then the few visitors that have been allowed in were restricted to the Kathmandu Valley, although a few Gurkha officers, namely

Bruce, travelled a little in the course of their duties. Even the British Resident, Brian Hodgson, during his decade there (1833–1843) was not allowed to travel, and Percival Landon, writing in 1928, estimated that as few as 130 Europeans had entered the Kathmandu Valley. During the years 1924–1927, but for a few small parcels, the whole of Nepal was mapped by the Survey of India, a remarkable achievement.

Nepal was still essentially feudal at the end of the 1940s, but a few visitors were being permitted beyond the confines of the valley into the middle hills. In 1948 a small group of Indian scientists was allowed to trace the route of the Bhote Khosi, and an American 'twitchers' group, led by Dr Dillon Ripley, collected birds in the hills of eastern and central Nepal. In that same year an expedition led by Dyhrenfuth visited the Nepal side of Kangchenjunga. In 1949 Nepal formally opened its doors to western mountaineers, by which time all other Himalayan countries, including Bhutan, had, in part at least, been explored. The 1949 expedition led by Tilman was not allowed to explore the Everest region as they had hoped; instead, they were permitted into Langtang and the eastern end of Ganesh, where they made the first ascent of Paldor. A Swiss expedition, including Rene Dittert and Dr Wyss-Dunant, reconnoitred Kangbachen in north-east Nepal that same summer.

Today, Nepal is so well and truly on the traveller's map that it is difficult to accept that the first expeditions were only allowed in less than half a century ago, and that from time to time the doors have had to close (1966–68) because of trouble on the borders. The first commercial trekking groups (organised by Jimmy Roberts) only came to Nepal in 1965 —

when the country had forty visitors including eight trekkers!

In spite of the inevitable changes — and there have been many over the past four decades — most of what is good about Nepal (and there is much) remains: the hills and flowers, the birds and wildlife, the culture and architecture, the mountains and rivers and, of course, the people. On the journeys in the chapters that follow I have had the opportunity to retrace my steps through a country that has become my passion. I have relived treks and expeditions along routes that have become 'classic', others that are 'off the beaten trek', and some that were new. My aim has not been to lead you in the arid language of the guidebook up the Buri, through the Khumbu or around Annapurna; there are several books already on the shelves which do that admirably. Instead I have tried to offer an insight into Nepal's landscape and culture — from its highest summits through its folded hills to the forested lowlands of the Terai — seen through the eyes of a fellow traveller. Hopefully my words will give you a feel for the place and perhaps motivate you to make similar journeys. Those already familiar with Nepal might be reminded of old pleasures and pointed towards new, and perhaps inspired to want to return. To that end I have included a brief 'fact sheet' at the end of each chapter that highlights the route, its difficulty and logistical problems so that, also using the maps, you can trace these expeditions and conjure up more. The final chapters give more general advice on rules and regulations, equipment, organization and where to find out further information. For armchair adventurers who ask the old question 'Why?', I hope the answer will become blatantly obvious.

Nepal still has much to offer the traveller in search of adventures for, although it has become more accessible, it remains in part, at least to the trekker and mountaineer, a forbidden kingdom. Areas such as Dolpo, Mustang, the north and west side of Dhaulagiri, north of Manang along the Nar Khola and the area north of Manaslu are all out of bounds to the trekker, although in several cases mountaineering expeditions are allowed through them to climb their mountain. One area fine trekking peaks and superb and demanding trekking was Rolwaling, closed for much of the last decade. The door to this high Sherpa enclave, west of the Khumbu in the shadow of Gauri Shankar, has just been reopened, as has that to the Kangchenjunga region in east Nepal, although at the moment only organized and self-contained trekking parties are admitted.

Finally, to all who would travel, I offer the words of Lord Curzon, made in a speech to the Royal Geographical Society in 1895:

In the first place consult all the highest and most reliable authorities you can find. In the second place read every book good bad or indifferent that has been written upon the country you propose to visit . . . In the third place take no superfluous baggage. In the fourth place realise that travel has not only its incidents and adventures but also its humour. And in the fifth place never expect any encouragement from the government of your country.

BILL O'CONNOR
Harrogate
May 1989

(Left) A tantric priest at Mani Rimdu during the swirling dance of the 'golden libation' makes an offering to Khumbu-yul-Lha the god protector of Khumbu.

Off the Beaten Trek:
Through Hinku and Hongu to Mera and Mingbo La

The most interesting parts of a map are the blank spaces. They are the spots I might explore some day . . . I make imaginary use of them.

Aldo Leopold

'Jani-ho — away you go,' sings John, belaying Sheila down the fixed rope.

Next the Sirdar, Ang Dorje, slides swiftly down the steep fluted snow using the fixed line without the safety rope. John is happy to descend the same way, only more slowly, since he doesn't have Sherpa lungs.

'See you at the bottom,' he states, before going hand over hand down the rope, kicking bucket steps in the snow.

Finally, I'm alone on the crest of the Mingbo La with the awesome block of Ama Dablam in front of me, whilst below icy flutings lead to the Nare Glacier where my party are spread like ink blots in the pristine snow. Looking eastwards across the desolate wastelands of the Hunku Nup Glacier, Baruntse and Makalu rise above the upper basin of the Hongu where the sacred lakes of Panch Pokhari are cradled in the arms of huge glacial moraines. Sad to leave it all behind, I untie the ropes from the snowbar and let them fall, snaking down the snow. Taking a final look around, I turn my back to the Hongu and descend to the glacier.

By the time we find a way through the seracs and crevasses of the glacier and set foot on the relative *terra firma* of moraine below the South Face of Ama Dablam, we are tired and burned from a long day in the sun and snow. I lie in my sleeping bag half out of the tent door, reading by the light of an almost full moon.

A Sherpa hurries across the moraine towards me. 'Burra Sahib come quickly, Ongchu big problem, plud shitting!' He grimaces, pushing out his tongue, pantomiming someone with an acute bout of Kathmandu Quickstep.

I follow him to the Sirdar's tent where Ongchu, our cook, is doubled up, shivering. Ang Dali, another Sherpa, is droning a mantra . . .

'What's the matter Dorje?'

'Ongchu has big pains and shitting blood,' he answers, matter of factly. 'He says he's going to die — same as Nima Tsering.'

Nima Tsering had been our cook on Himalchuli in 1978 and had died suddenly on trek after starting to pass blood, one of several Sherpa cooks who have died showing the same symptoms. I believe it to be stress-related. Expedition and trekking cooks work very hard trying to please their employers, a quality common to most Sherpas — they get up early to cook breakfast, and rush ahead to prepare lunch and buy fresh foods. At night they prepare good meals, often for large groups in rudimentary conditions, going late to bed after things have been cleared and perhaps preparing a packed lunch for the day ahead. On top of this, they have to trek and manage their finances. Compared to the Sherpa norm it represents a very stressful lifestyle.

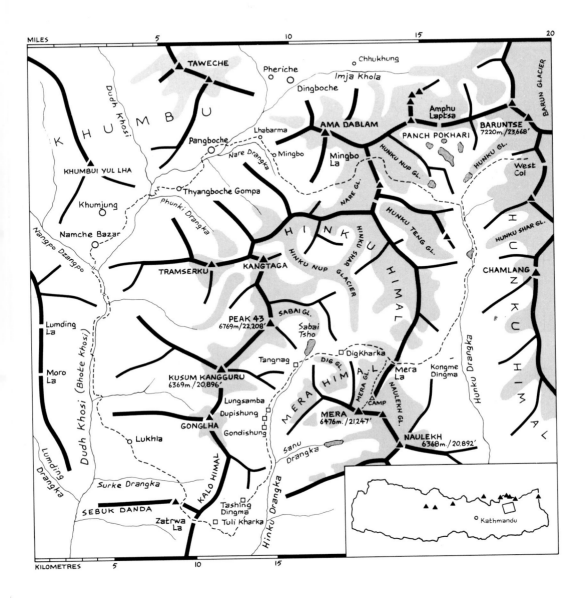

Horrified at Ongchu's condition I get Mike to have a look at him. Fortunately, I had three doctors on the trip, although one had got sick early on and had returned to Luklha. Mike was now the official trip 'sawbones'.

Mike examined the reluctant patient and took me aside, grim-faced.

'He's very sick — blood pressure's low and he's losing a lot of it.'

He explained what he thought was wrong; something about a perforated ulcer and what we could do for him with the equipment we had. As it happened we had an extensive medical kit as well as a brace of doctors. Mike called Hamish over for a second opinion — our cook was getting BUPA treatment on the National Health! The diagnosis was confirmed.

At the same time the 'alternative school of

11

The partly-frozen surface of a lake near our camp on the Hunku Nup Glacier (5,400m/17,712ft), reflects the massive bulk of Chamlang (7,290m/23,917ft) at the head of the wild Hongu basin. On the left is P4, on the right, Hongu Peak.

medicine' was in competition. Ongchu, looking helpless, was now being fed a bowl of rice and spicy lentil curry to maintain his strength, whilst another Sherpa chanted *Om mani padme Om*. The doctors wanted him to eat bland food, preferably milk-based, and lie flat with his feet raised. 'East is east and west is west and never the twain shall meet.' Pulling rank, I ordered a compromise which was reached with Ongchu eating milky boiled rice pudding. He was monitored through the night.

By the morning his condition had, if anything, worsened. Slowly we limped down to the huts at Mingbo below Ama Dablam, where Hillary had a base during the Silver Hut Expedition. Our dying Sherpa had refused to be carried.

Dorje explained his stubbornness. 'He thinks that if we carry him like a baby all his strength and spirit will go and then — gingerblut — dead.'

Meanwhile two other Sherpas had run ahead to Thyangboche Gompa to get a Lama to doctor both his body and spirit. At camp Ang Dali was burning juniper, producing a thick smoke for Ongchu to breathe. Our doctors, on the other hand, were preparing to administer a plasma drip and maintain his blood fluid levels, whilst I was fashioning a stretcher from tent poles, sleeping foams and climbing ropes.

Mike busied himself preparing a hypodermic. 'Bill, ask him to drop his trousers — he needs this.'

At the sight of the needle Ongchu definitely rallied, but submitted apathetically in the end! At which point the runners returned bearing two small red pills wrapped in dirty paper sent by the Lama. Ongchu received them in both hands, put them in his mouth and sucked slowly.

'What are they Dorje?'

'Medicine from Lama.'

'I know that,' I said impatiently, 'but what are they made from?'

He thought for a moment and answered patiently, 'Burra Sahib — that is Lama's secret but I think it comes from special plants mixed with water from his body.'

'Water from his body . . . do you mean . . .' I faltered, slightly lost for words, glancing at the horrified faces of the doctors. 'Surely you don't mean Lama . . . piss?'

'Lama piss very strong medicine,' replied the Sardar, with the nodded agreement of the other Sherpas.

It had been a worrying night. In the morning Ongchu was still with us, but the doctors agreed he was in a serious condition. The stretcher looked structurally sound and I instructed bearers on the correct method of carrying it. Protesting, the cook was tied on and carried down the moraines towards Pangboche. Just before the village he insisted, despite my bullying, that he would walk the rest of the way. We stayed the night in the lower settlement where Mike and Hamish continued treating him. Meanwhile, two more Lama Piss Smarties came up from Thyangboche, and he accepted them reverentially.

In the morning I went to see him. 'How are you feeling Ongchu?'

'Ramro Sahib — dherai ramro.'

He seemed to have made a miraculous recovery and insisted on walking to Thyangboche unaided. He wanted to give thanks to the Lama, and we wanted to see Mani Rimdu, the Tibetan-style dance drama held at the *gompa* at the time of the November full moon. Mike and Hamish warned him off hot foods, touching wood and keeping their fingers crossed for his eventual recovery. This was probably as effective as Lama's pills if you happen to be superstitious. The docs had done the best they could, so had the Lama. Each of us in our own mind knew whose medicine had worked in the battle of East and West . . .

Our trek had begun at Lukhla after the usual hairy flight from Kathmandu. We were a large party, intent on entering the Hinku Drangka east of the Dudh Khosi and climbing Mera (6,476m/21,247ft), highest of the nominated 'trekking peaks'. After this, weather permitting, we wanted to explore the upper Hongu Valley further east below Chamlang and Baruntse, before traversing the Mingbo La back into Khumbu — a wonderful journey through a wild, unspoiled region that few parties visit.

Climbing straight up from the airstrip, our first obstacle was the Kalo Himal, a ridge of rocky Alpine-scale peaks dividing the Dudh Khosi from the Hinku Drangka. Entering a steep forested cwm, drained by the Surke Drangka, I had already decided to take a couple of days acclimatizing before crossing the high Zatrwa La (4,600m/15,000ft).

The first Westerner to cross this pass and explore the Hinku and Hongu basins was J.O.M. Roberts with Sherpa Sen Tensing in May 1953. Roberts also made the first ascent of Mera, covering a route similar to the one we intended to follow. He then crossed back into Khumbu, but by the Amphu Laptsa, a difficult glacier pass that leads to the Imja Valley below Island Peak.

At the end of two days' exercise below the pass we were ready for pastures new. It was a steep climb to the Zatr Og, a notch on the Sebuk Danda that gives access to the pass. The rocky ground was mottled with low mounds of alpines finding rootspace in the thin soil, whilst the strange Himalayan Snowball plant, *Saussurea Gossypiphora*, looked like a ball of desiccated cobwebs. In fact it survives, despite the cold, by mummifying itself inside its own dead leaves and fibrous hairs.

'Hey, George, can you walk along that ridge and stand with the Sirdar; it's a great shot.'

George obliged and joined Ang Dorje on a rocky promontory overlooking the Dudh Khosi a vertical mile below.

'That's great — just look towards Numbur.'

Behind them the jagged moutainscape of the Lumding Himal filled the western horizon with Karyolung (6,511m/21,261ft), Khatang (6,853m/22,483ft), Teng Kang Poche (6,499m/21,322ft) and Kwangde Ri's crenelated summit ridge vying for dominance.

'Blimey Bill, hurry up — it's parky out 'ere.'

George was right; a cold wind was whipping over the ridge and I was taking too long to get the shot I wanted. We crossed the cairned col and descended into a rough boulder-filled valley to Tuli Kharka, used by herders from Pangkongma to the south during the monsoon. Below us the valley fell steeply away to the Hinku Drangka, soaring again from its wooded depths to the bulk of Mera (6,476m/21,247ft) and Naulekh (6,368m/20,892ft), ice-hung and glistening at the head of the Sanu Drangka, a tributary of the main river.

Both the Hinku and Hongu Valleys are without permanent settlements; their precipitous wooded flanks remain the preserve of Sherpa and Rai herders, and increasingly rare animals such as musk deer, *tahr* and perhaps the snow leopard. Hopefully they will remain so. Without settlements, all visiting groups need to be self-sufficient and responsible guardians of this beautiful environment. In the upper valleys the Arctic Alpine areas are even more fragile, and great care needs to be taken not to disturb the sensitive plants that are colonising the recently post-glacial landscape. In the future it might be necessary to protect these valleys under the umbrella of the Sagamartha National Park.

Still in deep shadow, we struck camp before traversing steeply around a spur into sunshine high above the flank of the Kote Zara. In several places the narrow trail had been washed out, where heavy rain had cut a gully, making it unstable and dangerous to cross. We eventually entered a forest of firs near the kharka of Tashing Dingma and descended to the river in sunlight, filtering through tall trees bearded with vivid grey-green Usnea lichen, making them seem older and more venerable somehow; like caricature Zen Masters from 'chop and kick' movies.

Extending northwards, the narrow valley was heavily wooded — fir, birch and rhododendron in a mixed tangle, reaching down to the river's edge. The path wound its way around boulders and fallen branches, climbing slowly to the gothes or huts, at Gondishung. Here a trilogy of summer pastures can be found that also include Dupishung and Lungsamba (4,063m/13,330ft), settled between the flanks of Kusum Kangguru (6,369m/20,896ft) and Mera; both officially trekking peaks.

'Om mani padme Om.' The sacred mantra of the Sherpa repeated over and over like the fingering of a rosary was our accompaniment up to the tiny *gompa* hidden above Gondishung.

'Very good *gompa* — you like see Burra Sahib.'

I agreed with Ang Dorje, I would like to see it.

'You lead the way — we can catch the rest up later.'

Several of the Sherpas wanted to see the *gompa* and joined the party on the climb up the hill. They chanted their rosary and collected aromatic leaves from tiny rhododendron. Built beneath a rock overhang, the *gompa* looked more like a hermit's retreat and I doubted whether it would be worth the effort. Once there, the Sherpas scrambled up to the building and opened the small door. Inside the room, really no more than a monk's cell, housed three large and surprisingly beautiful statues — a Buddha, and two Buddhsatvas, or possibly a Rhimpoche or head Lama. The Sherpas said that they had been brought from Tibet, but when was impossible to say. So much in Nepal that looks old has, in the language of the antiques trade, been 'distressed', so that relatively new objects look ancient. In a hearth near the altar the Sherpas made a fire of the leaves, which gave off a rich aromatic smoke that soon filled the cell and had me scurrying into the fresh outdoors.

Tangnag is a clutch of herders' huts at the head of the valley, set in a barren pasture beneath the inspiring south face of Peak 43 (6,769m/22,208ft), the eastern bastion of a knot of exquisite summits that make up the Kalo Himal and include Kusum Kangguru, Tramserku and Kangtaga.

'This will be a good place to spend a couple of days,' I tell Ang Dorje, who goes off to tell the cook our plans whilst we sit in the sun drinking sweet tea and scan the surrounding peaks for possible routes.

'That looks good,' enthuses John, pointing to the north-east face of Kusum Kangguru and he scribes a way up a black rock face etched with icy cracks. 'You could bivvi below the face and follow the thin couloir to below the hanging glacier.'

'Then what?'

'Well, then . . .'

Just as he was about to conceive the ultimate route, a block of ice, really the end of the hanging Tangnag Glacier, cleaved from the mass and seemed to hang in the air before smashing down the face and the imagined route, finally exploding over the sight of the proposed bivouac. It filled the air with disintegrating ice particles and the roar of its force. When our silence was broken, the comments about the route and John's eye for a line were profane.

Just behind camp to the north, huge moraines, like the mounds of ancient hill forts, hold back the waters of the Sabai Tsho, a turquoise jewel below the snout of the tumbling Sabai Glacier. Several of us spent part of the day walking here, watching small ice chunks break off into the lake to float as icebergs.

From Tangnag the valley turns abruptly east towards the Mera La. Following the lateral moraine of the Dig Glacier we camped just beyond Dig Kharka (4,731m/15,522ft), where the valley is joined by the Hinku Nup Glacier

A monk at Thyangboche blows a large conch shell horn.

valley from the north. Since we had given ourselves plenty of time and there was a need for more acclimatization, we stayed two nights at this camp. This gave us an opportunity to explore the valley to the north and also gave me a chance to hike over to the foot of the Mera La to see what lay ahead on the glacier.

In fact, the Mera La (5,415m/17,767ft) presented no great problems. A few awkward metres getting on to the glacier soon led to wide slopes and a slight ice ridge that rose in a sweeping arc towards the flat summit of the col. We placed Base Camp on the Hongu side about one hundred metres down in a gravel flat at the edge of the ice.

'Chiyah Sahib.' Lhakpa, the kitchen boy, rattles the icy nylon of my tent with the promise of Sherpa tea, hot, sweet and milky, its ingredients boiled together to make the beverage of the

Thrashing our way from the summit of Mera in a fury of wind and spindrift.

mountain gods. It's well worth making the Promethean effort of freeing an arm from the tropical interior of the sleeping bag to reach out for the steaming brew.

'*Tutche Lhakpa,*' I mutter, struggling to sit up. Shaking the sleep from my eyes releases a snowstorm that could be terminal dandruff but in fact is the frozen rime from a night's breathing falling from the tent. Outside it's a perfect morning. Everyone is standing around the cook tent — even in the wild a kitchen becomes a focal point of social gathering.

Soon after breakfast we climbed back to the col. Fewer now, we thread the wide crevassed slopes of the Mera Glacier in search of a suitable sight for a high camp. Most of the porters have been left behind; only the Sherpas equipped for the glacier help to carry loads. A perfect camp is eventually found by a rocky outcrop separating the Mera and Naulekh Glaciers. From a perch amongst the rocks the views are extensive — some of the best in Nepal.

Mera is the highest peak south of Everest in what might generally be termed the Khumbu Himal. From this vantage point an arc of mountains sweeps for a full 180 degrees, and includes many of Nepal's 8,000-metre giants as well as a host of smaller but no less spectacular summits. The panorama includes Numbur, Cho Oyu, the trilogy of Everest, Nuptse and Lhotse, then Makalu, Chamlang and, clearly visible to the east, the multi-summited Kangchenjunga.

I sat with George Fowler on the summit of the rocks. The others had retreated to their sleeping bags, psyching up for an early start and a summit bid in the morning. I had developed a great rapport with George. He always got the most from each day, being the last to bed and invariably first up in the morning. He would stand about in the cold rather than miss the sunrise, and was always ready to hare off and explore some mysterious corner or tricky boulder problem — ideal qualities on an adventurous trek like this.

When the alarm went off I was convinced that I hadn't been to sleep but had spent the night sifting thoughts and searching for a comfortable position. Thankfully, the Sherpas already had the brew on. Cook must have been up an hour or more and the primus was roaring. By the time everyone was up and dressed, struggling to put on gaiters and half-frozen boots, fumbling with harnesses and packing their rucksacks, breakfast was served — a mug of tea and a handful of glucose biscuits.

Rather than climb as a single team we tied on to two 50-metre ropes.

'Listen everyone — I'll lead the first rope, John the second. Keep the rope tight between each other and don't bother to carry coils or let it drag in the snow.' I intoned these safety reminders more to make sure everyone was alert to possible dangers rather than as instruction. 'Remember — slowly and try to keep in the tracks.' I led off, crunching a track through crusty snow.

Despite an inevitable reluctance to leave my sleeping bag I always enjoy night-time climbing — peering at grey shadows formed in my headtorch, trying to distinguish real from imagined holes, and charting the line on the ghostly bulk of the mountain ahead, grossly foreshortened under the colourless light of the stars. It's an unreal world; the asylum of mountaineers.

'Hold on a minute.'

A shout from the back of the line is carried forward on the wind. Instantly I jerk to a halt as the rope comes tight.

'My crampon's come loose.'

I stand still and realize how cold the night is and how sharp the wind feels as it dries the sweat on my neck. I close my eyes as a wave of tiredness sweeps over me and I feel I could sleep standing up. Five minutes later (it could have been an hour), I hear someone shout.

'OK, it's fixed — let's go.'

The route on the north side of Mera is straightforward — broad glacier slopes with only hidden crevasses to worry about. As we trudge up its gentle slopes I wish I had skis and could climb upwards on skins to the rhythmical push-drag cadence of ski mountaineering. By the time the sun appears we are well on our way to the East Summit but the slow dawn brings a fast cold wind. Worried by its chill I stop the party and make everyone pile on more layers. Even then it feels desperately cold, moving as slowly as we are towards the exposed col between Mera's summits . . .

What looked like the last few metres took over an hour to climb. The surface of the snow was crusted by the wind to the point that it almost took my weight but collapsed as I tried to transfer to the other foot, making every step a huge effort. Once on the col we split into two parties, with my rope going on to the higher summit. By the time we reached the North Summit we could see the others beginning their descent. The sky was still brilliantly clear so that even the most distant peaks were sharply defined, but the wind was building, and we could see that the dark rock pyramid of Everest had a huge snow plume arcing out over Tibet. In the hour or so it had taken us to retrace our steps to the col a full-blown gale now shot-blasted our exposed skin with spindrift making it impossible to walk into. Strangely, we could look up into an inky sky, yet ahead was a complete white-out. Already the track was impossible to see and in any case had blown over. Throwing caution to the wind we charged down the slope to escape the blizzard, stumbling over the crusty surface and searching desperately for a trace of bootprints. After a few hundred metres we dropped below the tempest and could clearly see the way ahead, and the rocky outcrop of the highcamp where the remaining Sherpas were packing up.

We didn't bother with a rest day after our summit success. Instead we had a leisurely breakfast in the sun before packing our gear and setting off on our exploration of the upper Hongu basin. Crossing a spur of the valley above Kongme Dingma, the enormous west flank of Chamlang dominated everything. By late afternoon we had reached the relatively flat valley floor of the Hongu and established a camp amongst boulders and coarse vegetation. Entering the Hongu after crossing the Mera La brings a sense of commitment. To be hit by a freak snowstorm now would mean a desperate struggle to get out safely. The trail south down the Hongu is difficult, involving a lot of ridge walking whilst crossing back over the Mera La is exposed and still leaves a lot of high trekking, either to recross to Lukhla or hike south via Mosum Kharka to Pangkongma. Northwards, only the Mingbo La and the Amphu Laptsa lead eventually to safety, but both are difficult crossings. The freak snowstorm that hit Nepal in October 1987 brought a halt to all of the expeditions in the Khumbu, including my own on Ama Dablam. Indeed, most people found it impossible to walk the well-used trails above Pangboche and many groups were marooned for several days in Pheriche, Lobuje and Gokyo. In the Hongu there are no hiding places or quick ways out. Much of the trekking is above 4,000 metres and often over 5,000 metres; porters in particular, less well equipped, are exposed to unacceptable dangers.

In the Hongu valley below the Hunku Shar Glacier was a frozen lake. We trudged slowly northwards over a dried silt flat along its eastern edge, where the mud had contracted into polygonal tiles so regular, it looked like a tiled floor. One member of the party who had done well on the summit day was now having trouble with her breathing. Her lungs were clear so we ruled out pulmonary oedema. Fortunately Sheila was stoic about her discomfort and responded in a couple of days to antibiotics, rest and lots of liquid. Again, the Hongu is no place to fall sick or become injured.

From a camp below the junction of the Hunku

Nup and Hunku glaciers we spent several days exploring towards the Amphu and West Col. This end of the valley is truly a mountain wilderness. Vast moraines form huge mounds on either side of the valley, whilst arcs of moraine dam the valley marking the terminus of the glacier's retreat.

In the evening we sat huddled with the Sherpas and porters, all Bhotes and all with expedition experience. Dressed in the equipment we had supplied to them — hats, gloves, socks, boots, jackets and thick wool trousers, many of them a scruffy fit — they looked a poor lot; an image which belied the truth. In fact, a finer bunch would be hard to find and my memories of that small army are as fond and as vivid as any I hold. Before leaving the warmth of the huddle I told the Sirdar our plans and gave instructions about food.

'Tomorrow, Dorje, several of us will make an early start to hike towards West Col and Panch Pokhari — get Ongchu to make up some packed lunches; biscuits, chapattis, that kind of thing.'

He gave the standard reply of the long-suffering Sirdar.

'No problem.'

The kitchen boy came over with a couple of 'chota pegs' of hot butter *rakshi*, a favourite tipple of mine in highland Nepal and the perfect antidote to a frosty night. We continued talking about expeditions. He had twice been to the top of Everest and had climbed Ama Dablam and a handful of other important summits.

'By the way, Ang Dorje,' I asked, before turning in, 'how long before Mani Rimdu at Thyangboche?'

'One week, Burra Sahib.'

Panch Pokhari ('five lakes'), is a cluster of sacred lakes below the Amphu Laptsa (5,780m/ 18,963ft), held tight behind the rocks of the Hinku's glaciers. Five is an auspicious number, especially amongst lakes, and the traveller in Nepal will find many 'Panch Pokharis',

Ging-pa, the guardian king of the North, dancing during Mani Rimdu.

regardless of the fact that there may be four, five or, in this case, eight readily countable oases. We walked separately along the narrow moraine crest, selfishly savouring this barren wilderness and isolation. Little seems to grow on these raw unstable moraines; blotches of orange lichen and a few sparse alpines are all that can take hold in the soilless slopes.

The lateral moraine of the Hunku Glacier sweeps in a crescent eastwards towards Baruntse (7,220m/23,688ft), which forms a mountain divide between the Hongu and the Barun at the head of the Arun drainage system. By following the moraine, which eventually gives way to snow slopes and glacier, a col south of Baruntse, West Col (6,135m/20,128ft), leads to the Lower

Barun Glacier and in turn to Sherpani Col (6,110m/20,046ft), which provides access to the base of Makalu.

We moved camp to the edge of the Hunku Nup Glacier at about 5,400 metres (17,712ft), close to a lake at its snout. Covering the ice were huge, square-cut, pale granite boulders, eroded remnants of the Mingbo Peaks. The partly frozen surface of the lake amplified the blue-green of the ice and sky, reflecting the image of the massive north face of Chamlang (7,290m/23,917ft) and its endless east-west summit ridge. Our journey to this lake had not been without difficulty, so finding small shrines of stones with strings of dried orange chrysanthemums and a tiny prayer bell on a granite block by the lakeside, we had to admire the Sardhu's progress whose pilgrimage had brought him so far.

Camped on the ice it felt the coldest night yet. The porters were crammed into a large base tent wrapped in everything we could find whilst the Sherpanis happily slotted in between the Sherpas — kith with kin! At dawn we packed quickly, and ascended the stepped ice to broad slopes that swept gently towards the curve of the Mingbo La, beyond which the top third of Ama Dablam peeked like a glistening crystal. Ang Dorje forged ahead whilst I brought on the slow ones. Even Ongchu, normally ahead of the pack, was making heavy weather of it and I joked with him about too much hot *rakshi*. By the time I reached the col the Sirdar had fixed a rope down the steep fluted west side and the first of the porters had already descended. I fixed another rope to speed up the descent and gradually, two by two, we left the Hongu behind, until only Sheila, John, the Sirdar and myself were left on the col . . .

At Thyangboche Gompa the people of the Khumbu were gathering for Mani Rimdu. Plenty of trekkers also attend this three-day dance drama where good does battle with evil;

gods and demi-gods are paraded and appeased, whilst mortals receive the blessing of the Rinpoche, Passang Tensing.

I waited patiently with the others, in line behind the Sirdar and Ongchu, holding a prayer scarf in both hands ready to present it to the Rinpoche. I was a little nervous, unsure of the form, and I pushed the Sherpas ahead so I could see how to give the *kata* and receive the blessing. Ang Dorje could sense my worry and turned, saying, 'No problem, Burra Sahib — do same as me.'

When my turn came I presented my scarf to the Rinpoche. He took it and placed it around my neck, then, to my horror, he gave me two red pills! The Sherpas had eaten theirs, but I palmed mine like a card sharp. Into my other hand a monk poured milky liquid which looked like *chang*, and which I slurped automatically as the others had done before me. Looking to the Sirdar to see what came next, I noticed he was smiling.

'That, Burra Sahib, was *very* strong medicine!'

ITINERARY:

DAYS 1 – 3: KATHMANDU TO TULI KHARKA

Fly to Lukhla from Kathmandu. Cross the Zatrwa La and descend on the Hinku side to Tuli Kharka.

It is also possible to walk from Jiri and enter the Hinku from the south via Pangkongma, but this takes considerably longer.

DAYS 4 – 6: TULI KHARKA TO TANGNAG

Descend to Tashing Ongma and follow the Hinku Drangka north through summer pastures at Gondishung, Dupishung and Lungsamba to Tangnag.

DAYS 7 – 8: TANGNAG TO KHARE

Explore the upper Hinku. Camps at Dig Kharka and Khare below the Mera La. Those wishing to climb Mera would be advised to spend more time acclimatizing before going up it.

DAY 9: KHARE TO BASE CAMP

Cross Mera La and site Base Camp 100 metres down on east side of pass. Those not wishing to climb Mera Peak should continue to Kongme Dingma.

DAYS 10 – 12: CLIMB MERA PEAK

Establish High Camp. Continue to summit, descend to High Camp or Base Camp.

DAYS 13 – 15: BASE CAMP TO PANCH POKHARI

Descend into Hongu, explore northwards to Amphu/Panch Pokhari. Wild and wonderful scenery.

DAYS 16 – 17: CROSS MINGBO LA

Establish camp on Hunku Nup Glacier and cross Mingbo La. Camp below Nare Glacier and Ama Dablam. Spectacular.

DAY 18: MINGBO TO PANGBOCHE

Descend moraines to Pangboche. Small kharka old airstrip.

DAYS 19 – 21: PANGBOCHE TO LUKHLA

Descend via Thyangboche and Namche to Lukhla. Most parties will prefer more time exploring the Sherpa villages.

DIFFICULTY:

This is a strenuous and serious trek into an area without habitation. The ability to be self-sufficient is essential. In the case of accident or poor weather, retreat would be difficult. Mera Peak by its normal route offers little in the way of technical difficulty but it is high (6,476m/ 21,242ft). Much of the trekking in Hongu is above 5,000 metres (16,400ft). The Mingbo La is a glacier pass with a steep west flank. There is also crevasse danger on the Nare Glacier.

LOGISTICS:

The quickest way into the area is to fly to Lukhla. Walking in from Jiri and entering Hinku from the south will add about ten days. It is essential to engage hill porters, preferably Sherpas, Tamangs or Rai, and vital that they are equipped to spend time above snow level and have suffcient food and shelter for the duration of the expedition.

EQUIPMENT:

Specialist mountaineering equipment is required, with mountain boots rather than normal lightweight trekking boots, and gaiters and down clothing, even for those not intending to climb Mera. Ropes, ice axes, crampons and snow bars and ice screws will be needed. Sherpas and porters will require a fixed rope down from the Mingbo La, and porters will require snow goggles, shoes and additional warm clothing. For more information on Mera Peak see *Trekking Peaks of Nepal* by Bill O'Connor (Crowood Press, 1989).

SEASON:

Post-monsoon is the ideal time to go, although it is much colder at night. November seems to be particularly reliable. Care should be taken in

Jani-ho, away you go! — down the fluted west flank of the Mingbo La into Khumbu.

the spring not to go in too early — late April through May seems satisfactory.

MAPS:

The Hongu and Hinku, like the rest of the Everest region, are well and truly mapped. Apart from a very good RGS 1:50,000 (now, alas, not available), there are two Schneider 1:50,000 maps for the area — the Khumbu Himal and Shorong/Hinku sheets.

Last Virgin in the Khumbu:
People, peaks and villages of the Khumbu

The Birth of Sagamartha

Before the formation of the continents, there appeared in the sky a cloud the size of the universe. From this cloud rain fell continuously for ages. This rainwater remained suspended in space, kept there by the force of the wind, which also kept it from dispersing in the sky. The winds blowing from all directions churned the surface of this suspended body of water, causing the agglomeration of its molecules into a solid mass which grew higher and higher, rising from the surface as the water level receded. The waves slapping at its sides became glaciers and snow falling above turned it white. Thus was formed the Queen of mountains; Sagamartha, the crown jewel of the earth.

Gyeshe O.D. Vajar

Descending from Mendelphu Hill above Namche Bazar, I pass a line of heavily-laden yaks, grunting and overheated with the effort of the climb, lolling open-mouthed, their purple tongues extended to taste the thin, cold air. Unhurried, they grind their teeth on imaginary cud, encouraged on by a Sherpa who gives a shrill call and skilfully aims small stones at their hairy flanks.

Seen from the hill, Namche, the trading capital of the Khumbu, crowned by the Sagamartha Park Headquarters, is not unlike a classical Greek theatre. Built in an open-ended hollow above the Bhote Khosi, its stone-built, two-storey *khangba* (houses) form concentric terraced rows, separated by little more than handkerchief-sized yards bound by dry-stone walls, highlighting only too well the shortage of land that exists in the community. In recent years, the growing demands of tourism and the prosperity it brings have led to the building of larger and more sophisticated lodges, to compete with the patchwork of dirt squares below the town which alternate between potato field and campground with the seasons.

In town, sitting on the terrace of a trekkers' lodge at the end of the main street, we order the first glass of what has become an endless demand for hot, sweet tea. Lounging opposite, my burned-brown companions pick from a huge bowl of *rigi* (potatoes), a staple amongst the Sherpa. Boiled in their skins they are clenched in the hand and peeled with the thumb, in the local fashion, before the creamy flesh is dipped into a small dish of *korsani* (hot sauce) and eaten. Reluctant to leave the Khumbu at the end of our expedition, we relax in the carefree morning sun watching the Khumbu's world go by.

A group of pale pink trekkers, fresh from Lukhla, wander up the cobbled main street. Stopping at most of the stores, more to rest than to bargain, they climb the stone steps, wobbly-kneed, between stone houses, in pursuit of the heavily-laden yaks. Breathing hard, they are only too aware that it has taken them little over a day's hiking and a forty-minute flight to come

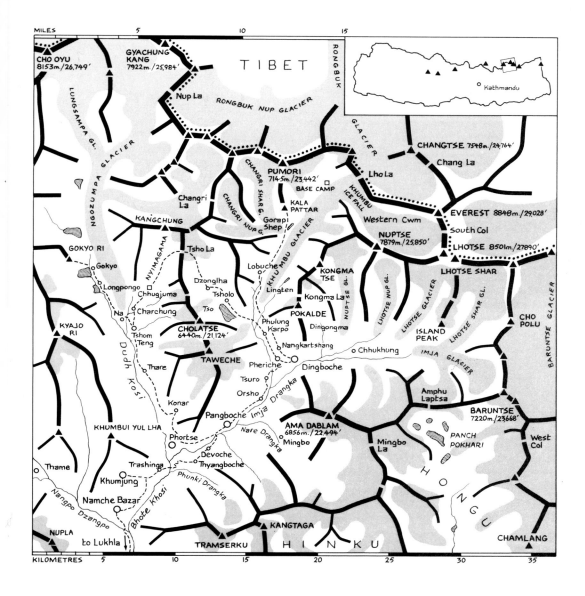

from Kathmandu to the Sherpa capital at 3,446 m (11,306ft). They will be wise and probably content to spend a day or so acclimatizing in and around Namche before exploring the valleys and villages beyond, or making the pilgrimage to Everest Base Camp or Kala Pattar.

Today the Everest Expedition Route, or at least part of it, is one of the most sought-after treks in Nepal. Since the route was pioneered in

the early 1950s inevitable changes have occurred, making the Solu/Khumbu much more accessible. However, the trek to Everest remains one of the richest in terms of scenery, culture and ultimate physical achievement for those who want to cross high passes and reach small summits and viewpoints like Gokyo Ri and Kala Pattar. What the trek to Everest is not, although you can look out over vast mountain wastes, is a

At the head of the valley beyond Thyangboche gompa only the massive southern ramparts of the Lhotse-Nuptse wall and the summit pyramid of Sagamartha, the Mother of the Universe, are burnished bronze by sunset.

'wilderness experience'. The trek through the foothills of Nepal along traditional trade routes brings you into close contact with its varied people — from Newars, Tamangs and Rai to Sherpas and Tibetans — against a backcloth of mountains that extends from the Jugal through Gauri Shankar, and other Rolwaling peaks, to Everest and beyond. This cultural diversity in a land where 'men and mountains meet', is for me part of the richness of trekking in Nepal.

Although it's still possible to follow most of the original route from Kathmandu, perhaps beginning the walk at Dholalghat, a Swiss-built extension off the Chinese road now goes to Jiri from Lamasangu, shortening the trek by several days. Other 'jet-trekkers' with even less time to spare fly to the STOL airstrip at Lukhla. Ultimately, of course, the benefits of taking the long route in, be it from Dholalghat or Jiri, are manifold. The most obvious advantage is that you have time to adjust to the rhythms and pace of Nepal, at the same time becoming both fit and acclimatized for the high country ahead.

But for most travellers the lasting gain is through contact with the landscape and people as they traverse the country's grain from west to east, passing from ridge to valley through a multitude of villages.

For so long the forbidden Kingdom of Nepal remained a mystery to western explorers long after other Himalayan countries had revealed their secrets. Mount Everest, named after Sir George, the Surveyor General of India from 1830 to 1843, had for several decades attracted British expeditions who approached the mountain through Tibet, the only route of access. All but yielding to the efforts of Mallory and Irving in 1924, Chomolungma, as the Tibetans call the mountain, remained unclimbed until Nepal opened her borders. Within a few years a way was found, via the Sherpa homeland of the Solu/Khumbu and Namche Bazar, to the foot of the mountain and the start of a feasible route. The way into the Western Cwm to the South Col was pioneered by the Swiss in 1952. Finally in 1953, a British

24

expedition, led by John Hunt, succeeded in putting New Zealand mountaineer Edmund Hillary and Sherpa Tensing Norgay on the highest summit in the world.

By the time those trekkers who have walked in from Jiri reach Namche, they have been on the trail for seven or eight days, and have covered well over one hundred miles with close on 60,000 feet of ascent and descent; for them, the climb up Mendelphu Hill is barely noticeable.

Our expedition had come to the area over a month before to climb Cholatse (6,440m/ 21,124ft), the last virgin in the Khumbu. The small Anglo-American team was led by Dr Peter Hackett, who had run the HRA hospital in Pheriche for eight years, and undoubtedly knew a thing or two about Khumbu virgins. The year before, I had met him wheezing his way from Base Camp after the successful ascent of Everest during the American Medical Research Expedition of 1981. As well as Peter, the team included Vernon Clevinger, a blond-haired, blue-eyed Californian rock-jock whom I had first met in Kathmandu — his huge frame and bulging biceps would have made him equally at home on a mountain or at Malibu. 'The Hulk', as he became known, was our secret weapon — if we couldn't climb the mountain, he could pull it down! Galen Rowell was no stranger to the Khumbu, and as America's leading mountain photographer and author he had climbed extensively in the Himalaya. John Roskelley, a late and very welcome addition to the team, was regarded by many as the foremost Himalayan mountaineer in the USA. His record at that time was second to none, but his outspoken approach to climbing and its problems was often at odds with others in his country, where a more laid-back approach is the norm. However, in a debate where actions speak louder than words, John would win the vote. I wasn't surprised to find out that his mother hailed from Yorkshire, and as the only Brit in the team I was glad to co-opt the 'little tyke' during normal expedition banter.

Galen was unable to join us straight away, since he was busy shepherding a group of 'mail-order mountaineers' in the wilderness on a photographic safari, so the rest of us set off on a trek of our own before going to the mountain.

From Namche, Peter headed up to Khumjung to visit a Sherpa child whom he had adopted after the father had been killed. The rest of us headed towards Thyangboche on the trail that contours high above the west bank of the Imja Drangka. Above and far below forests still remain, whilst the path gently rises and falls across open hillside, cropped by grazing and heady with the scent of the dwarf rhododendron, whose oily aromatic leaves are burned as incense during prayer. Berberis and clumps of alpines create a vivid foreground to a stunning ice-hung backdrop dominated by the sacred summit of Ama Dablam. Seen across the deep azure shadow of the Imja Gorge, its relatively modest height seems enhanced beyond its loftier neighbours. After the dust and bustle of the bazaar this bright, open hiking puts a spring in the step and Sanasa is soon reached. Here the higher trail from Khumjung descends through huge boulders and forest to a collection of t-shops and stalls run by friendly, sharp-witted Tibetans. Some of these people undoubtedly stayed in the area after four thousand or so refugees crossed over the Nangpa La at the end of the 1950s, following the Chinese invasion and occupation of their country.

Peter rejoined us at the t-shop where the arrival of the good doctor was an excuse for the locals to hand round *chang*, a milky millet or rice beer. Several were supped before we were allowed to continue our descent through fir forest to Trashinga and the bridge at Phunki Tenga. Wary of house calls with Peter we avoided the t-shops over the bridge, and passing the water-driven mani-wheels clacking their mantras to the wind, we wound our way for six hundred long metres up the heavily-forested spur separating the Imja and Phunki rivers, to Thyangboche.

Built at the foot of Kangtaga and Tramserku, the monastery is a spectacular vantage point, with extensive views into the major Khumbu valleys and of many of its mountains — a good place for the shepherd to watch over his flock! Despite its apparent antiquity, the main building dates only from the mid-1930s; the original *gompa*, built around 1915, was destroyed by an earthquake. Like much that you see in Nepal, weather, work and woodsmoke have brought on premature ageing.

(As I finish this book, having just returned from the Khumbu, the *gompa* now stands sadly as a blackened ruin, reminiscent of the Tibetan monasteries after the Chinese destruction. In this case a fire appears to have been caused by a heater powered by an electric generator, which was installed recently to take the pressure off wood burning.)

A traditionally-dressed Sherpani in Namche Bazar.

By late morning, as often happens in the spring months, it clouded over, but as normal in the evening the peaks cleared. I wandered past the main buildings, westwards along the crest of the spur beyond a new lodge, to a point where I could look back over a coppice of rhododendrons, birch and red berberis to the pagoda-like roof of the *gompa*, dominated by the seemingly omnipotent form of Ama Dablam. Gradually, the sun left the nearby summits until, north-east at the head of the valley, only the summit pyramid of Sagamartha ('Mother of the Universe'), reflected the sun's heat like burnished bronze. Finally that too blackened, so that only the ephemeral crystals of its snow plume flickered, like a candle's flame, before the day died.

The cold night was spent in warm company at the Mountain Travel Lodge. We slept soundly until dawn, when droning, flatulent blasts from the *dung-chen*, the telescopic horns several metres long used in Buddhist ceremony, rudely heralded the new day. As we made ready to leave, *thawa* (monks), two by two, beating drums with curved sticks, blowing shrill, reeded horns and loud trumpets, accompanied by others with crashing cymbals and clanging bells, paraded by. In a cacophony of discordant sound to ward off evil, rather than as musical messengers of the divine, they trooped up the ridge to a propitious place for prayer.

We continued towards Everest, past the nunnery at Devoche, and through an almost mystical forest, of Himalayan birch with its peeling papery bark, silver fir and large rhododendrons, draped with tattered Usnea lichen fluttering like natural prayer flags to the *shing-lhu* (forest spirit). We must have had good karma because that morning we surprised both pheasants and musk deer before we reached the bridge, a swaying raft of planks, suspended over the Imja's gorge and providing a stunning vista of Ama Dablam. Sadly, such forests are fast thinning in the Khumbu, where many lodges build huge fires to keep trekkers warm, boil water for their showers and cook wildly elaborate menus. The kitchen in the *gompa's* lodge is particularly bad, and the fall of the woodsman's axe is a constant reminder of the dwindling reserves and diminishing returns of such an economy.

Now on the true right bank of the Imja the path climbs to a *chorten* (Buddhist shrine), whose shape symbolically represents earth, water and fire along with the thirteen steps of enlightenment and the natural forces of wind and sun. As with the *mani*-walls, we pass, keeping it to the right out of respect for the religious offering enshrined within it.

A little further on a *kani* (archway), decorated with religious paintings, close to some huge boulders, marked a notch in the trail where the way divided. The left-hand path climbed to upper Pangboche (3,985m) whilst the other contoured to the lower settlement. We took the higher route in order to revisit the ochre-walled *gompa* in the upper village, said to have been founded some three hundred years ago by Lama Sangwa Dorje, the patron saint of the Sherpa. His hand print (*pang*) can be found on a rock near the *gompa*, which is set in a spinney of ancient, gnarled junipers. The main building (which no longer has resident monks) was locked, but knowing the form we sent for the keeper of the keys who lives nearby. An old Sherpani eventually returned, carrying a large iron key, and opened the equally huge padlock on the main door. Inside, dusty light filtered in to reveal two low benches leading to the main altar on which were numerous Buddha-like statues. On either side, grimy parcels of cloth contained religious texts bound between wooden boards. The walls were covered in religious paintings, whose iconography seemed too complicated and confused to be explained, but the real treasures of the *gompa* were housed upstairs.

A stairway outside led to an upper room with more icons and *thankas* (religious scroll paintings). A large iron-bound chest was opened, and what looked like a cigar box along with another package removed. Slowly, with reverence and all the stagecraft of a magician, they were revealed. In the one was a skeletal hand held together by the arid remnants of its flesh and sinews, and in the other a conical skull-cap of coarse red hair — both, we were told, were from the Yeti!

After leaving the normal token of our appreciation, we joined the main trail passing

A monk at Thyangboche gives a flatulent blast on the dung-chen.

27

long *mani*-walls. On the far side of the valley a tributary, the Nare Drangka, has gouged a deep channel through the moraines near Mingbo. This was caused in 1977 when a moraine lake below Ama Dablam burst, sending a flood of water down the valley which destroyed both bridges and life.

Such catastrophes and awful displays of nature seem the norm in the mountains. After the 1977 flood Ed Hillary and various other aid organizations set to and built larger suspension bridges, and greatly improved the route between Lukhla and Namche. The Austrians also installed an HEP scheme below Thami to bring power and light to the main villages. However, on 5 August 1985, a lake above Thami burst from the moraine, causing a massive wall of water to flood down the Bhote Khosi, destroying much of the Austrian scheme and washing away all of the bridges to Phakding.

At Orsho, where the trail to Dingboche follows a meander of the Imja Khola to the right, we took a left-hand path which climbs past Tsuro to crest the moraine and descend to the bridge before entering the dusty, intricately-walled Pheriche. A cold and windy place beneath mammoth lateral moraines deposited by the Khumbu Glacier and looked over by the twinned peaks of Cholatse and Taweche, it is really the last Sherpa settlement before Everest Base Camp. It must be said that in recent years Lobuje, once little more than two desolate stone huts, has expanded to meet the demands of trekkers.

For Peter, an authority on high altitude medicine, Pheriche is work and home, since the HRA hospital provides him with both. During the season a constant throughput of trekkers with headaches and injuries visit the hospital for

(Preceding page) A Sherpani preparing a meal inside a summer goth *(hut) in the kharka below Cholatse.*

help, advice and drugs, and in Peter's time to listen to a solar-powered Bob Marley! For the next few days Pheriche provided us with a base from which to explore and photograph the upper Khumbu.

In half light, just as the stars were fading, I climbed the moraine behind the village and watched the sunrise touch the icy flanks of Taweche and Cholatse, the mountain that in a few days we hoped to climb. From the moraine crest I looked at a circle of peaks that included the massive unclimbed south face of Lhotse (8,501m/27,890ft), Nuptse (7,879m/25,850ft) and Pumori (7,145m/23,442ft), Mallory's Daughter Peak, the ice-hung obelisk of Ama Dablam (6,856/22,493ft), and the distant eight-thousanders, Cho Oyu (8,153m/26,749ft) and Makalu (8,475m/27,805ft). Each in its turn, as altitude or position dictated, literally came to life as the dawn brought changes in colour and shadow, making them appear to stretch and twist awake in the morning sun.

From the moraine crest I had the choice either to climb to Nangkartshang Gompa above Dingboche, or descend past the chorten to the village itself for whatever breakfast I could find. Being strong-willed I resisted the temptation to visit the *gompa* and descended for tea and tatties.

Although I had initially intended to have a tough day, I had an attack of what Tilman called 'mountaineer's foot' — the inability to put one in front of the other! What I had intended this time (and actually did on another trek) certainly makes for a more adventurous journey. It involves a crossing of the Kongma La (5,535m/18,159ft), a rocky pass between the official 'trekking peaks' of Pokalde (5,806m/19,048ft) and Kongma Tse (5,820m/19,094), to Lobuje. A reasonable route leads from yak at Dingongma above Dingboche to some small tarns on the east side of the pass, and then to the rough pastures near Lingten amongst moraines east of the Khumbu Glacier. A way can then be found across the rubble-covered ice to and from the lodges at Lobuje.

From Lobuje most trekkers intent on reaching Everest Base Camp or Kala Pattar, the 'black-hill' above Gorak Shep, make a pre-dawn start and follow the trail north-east, crossing the mound of the Changri Glacier to the sandy flat of Gorak Shep. From here there are two options: you can climb the 300 metres (1,000ft) to the summit of Kala Pattar, which is really an extension of the south ridge of Pumori, and provides one of the most stunning viewpoints of the Everest group imaginable. Alternatively, you can continue to the site of Everest Base Camp at the foot of the Lho La and the Khumbu ice fall; although it means walking on the rubble-covered Khumbu Glacier. This involves no technical mountaineering and is a route often followed by yak trains during large expeditions. Only the very fit and fast could do both in the day without having a night over at Gorak Shep, where there is simple accommodation and camping. This is certainly the best option as it allows you to be on the 5,545-metre (18,188ft) summit for dawn or sunset.

After our stay at Pheriche, we returned down the valley to Phortse by traversing the steep hillside on the opposite side of the Imja to Thyangboche. We arrived late in the village after spending several hours stalking a large herd of Tahr *en route*.

Joined by our Sirdar Ang Nima, and a train of yaks and zubziok, we followed the path high above the true left bank of the Dudh Khosi through the *yersas* (summer pastures) of Konar, Thare and Tshom Teng. Following vague paths, we climbed the hillside eastwards to meadows in a hanging valley. Here, below the tumbling glaciers on the west face of Cholatse (Jobo Lhaptsan on the Schneider Khumbu map), we established our Base Camp.

On an unclimbed mountain you can be spoilt for choice. The South Ridge obviously

Hairy-flanked yaks — the alternative transport of the Khumbu.

presented the easiest option but it lacked a strong line, whilst the North-East Face had obvious lines but appeared to present the most difficulty. In the end we went for the South-West Ridge because it seemed to offer both an aesthetic line and acceptable difficulty.

Galen was still adrift so we set to and established an equipment dump below the West Face, which gave us a chance to take a close look at the problems. The first one was to establish a camp somewhere on the ridge from which to make a continuous lightweight ascent of the mountain. Over the next four days this was done, with the major difficulties being a mini Khumbu icefall, and a steep snow and ice headwall leading to a col at the foot of the ridge. Having achieved this we returned to base to await the prodigal's arrival so that we might have our full complement of climbers for the ascent.

With Galen came the bad weather; three days of snowfall left us with the options of waiting, reading, sleeping and eating. We did them all until despondency overcame inertia and we set off for Gokyo Ri.

Crossing the headwaters of the Dudh Khosi at Na, we followed the main trail along the lateral moraines on the true right bank of the

31

The trek through the Imja Valley beyond Thyangboche is dominated by the omnipotent form of Ama Dablam.

Ngozumpa Glacier, the largest in the Khumbu. From the turquoise lake at Longpongo, where a small flotilla of 'ruddy shell duck', on migration from Tibet were resting, we continued to Dudh Pokhari, a higher moraine lake at Gokyo. A herder's hut in an exquisite position provided refreshment before we made the 600-metre ascent to the cairned summit of Gokyo Ri. This, along with Kala Pattar and Poon Hill on the Annapurna trek, is one of the most outstanding viewpoints in Nepal which is attainable without technical climbing. For a full 360 degrees you can see endless mountains, from Numbur and Menlungtse in the south and west to Everest and

climbing to Col Camp, leaving Ang Nima to look after base. During the night Peter became sick, leaving us with no option but to continue without him; a miserable decision.

Above, the ridge became increasingly difficult, and was made more so by the heavy packs required for our lightweight ascent! At the end of a long day's ice climbing we emerged on to a rocky pinnacle, beyond which was a minute icy hollow overhanging an immense drop to the Gyalagba Glacier. Whilst Vernon and I hacked tent platforms and brewed, Galen and John prepared the ridge ahead, leaving our climbing ropes in place for a rapid start in the morning. Deciding that the climbing was too difficult for such heavy loads we agree to leave the tents and try to make the summit in a single push.

In the tent we talk and brew whilst outside it snows. 'It's gonna be hard', says John, in his thoughtful drawl. 'The ridge is out so it looks as though we'll have to climb diagonally below it ... above the south face buttress ... real wild if you come off.' As an afterthought he adds, 'You're out over the overhangs.'

At last, a comfortable position, found too late as digital bleeps mean it's time to go. Pre-dawn fumbling, trying to get dressed in the chaos of the tent, suppressing nausea, drinking a tepid fruit drink and packing, before, robot-like, we haul ourselves upwards on the fixed ropes. Off-balance moves around icy bulges, peering into unfathomable depths through steamed-up glasses are as scary as hell.

By the time we reach the end of the ropes, rhythm and commitment return and I begin to look forward to the route ahead.

Confident and fast, Roskelley side-steps the steepening ramp above me, hooking his axe around an icicle to make a layaway move and gain another step. A score of rope lengths later the way on is barred by a wall of seracs which we scour, from a rocky perch, looking for a line of weakness. Difficult climbing up an icy rift is followed by two more almost vertical pitches

Makalu in the east, to say nothing of the nearest neighbours, Cho Oyu, (8,153m/26,749ft) and Gyachung Kang (7,922m/25,991ft) due north. For us of course nothing was finer than the sparkling tooth of Cholatse in a fresh coating of snow under a true blue dream of a sky.

The following day we were back in the fray,

leading to a horizontal platform on top of the barrier. It begins to snow.

Taking stock, we agree to leave our sacks whilst we make a dash for the summit. In a white-out I lead off quickly, to be halted by an abyss; a huge crevasse separates the serac from the ridge ahead. John eventually finds a slither of ice bridging the gap and crawls across. Climbing the icewall opposite, we gain the summit plateau. Unseen, the way ahead unfolds until bulging ice has to be climbed direct to a gash like a sabre's cut. From its shelter a final pitch leads to a narrow ridge dividing the south and west faces of the mountain.

Reduced to dog-paddle by depth hoar we caterpillar towards the final pyramid, revealed at last as the clouds clear. Almost too late, exposed to the full fury of the wind and spin-drift, we edge along the crest to lose a dream by gaining the unclimbed summit.

After too brief a moment on the top, we slip, slide and abseil back down as the storm gathers its second wind. Diving across the schrund from its upper lip we regain our rucksacks and prepare for an open bivouac at 6,400m (21,000ft). Insidiously the snow finds gaps in sleeping bag and clothing until, after a long night of clenched teeth shivering, I'm aware of a pallid dawn.

After endless horrifying abseils, many of them diagonal, some from snow mushrooms, we arrive at the tents weary and parched, as much from fear as from effort. We brew and pack before the final, airy descent to Peter, whom we had left at the col. Already a day overdue we knew he would be worried and hungry! Not knowing that Peter had stayed behind, those at Base had seen four of us during the clearing near the summit and had drawn the wrong conclusion.

By the time we reached him it was snowing again. Obviously disappointed, he passed around some warm liquid. We cleared the camp leaving the col for the last time, to descend apprehensively through the icefall.

We decided to have our celebrations in hospital. Leaving the Sirdar to transport the loads to Namche we set off on the high route over the Thso La (5,420m/17,782ft), a glacier pass connecting the Dudh Khosi with the Khumbu Valley. An enjoyable and scenic crossing, often used by competent trekking groups, it is difficult to find and follow in cloudy conditions.

With Galen I set off early for the pass, wanting to make the most of the clear weather for photography. By the time we reached Charchung and had entered the Nyimagama Valley, cloud was billowing from below up the Dudh Khosi. A dusting of snow covered the ground, obliterating previous tracks. By the time we reached Chhugjuma we were walking in cloud. Without a compass or map we continued, relying on memory to find the pass, and were soon hopelessly lost. However, with fresh snow and now rime caused by the freezing cloud, we idled our time taking moody images, hoping the others would catch us up. Meanwhile we followed animal tracks, hoping to spot their maker. One set of prints, which we took to be those of a dog, went purposefully up the valley and we followed. Skilfully winding its way across the moraines the dog seemed to be linking cairns. With all sense of direction gone we blindly pursued our leader. Climbing a scree slope I recognized a boulder under which I had previously bivouacked. We were beneath the pass.

Ascending from right to left, still following our canine guide, we reached the edge of the ice, where it was obvious the trail continued across the glacier-covered pass. Still in thick mist, we traversed a perfect line in the footprints of our unseen friend, descending the far side by a series of cairned, snow-covered rocky terraces. And so it went on, to Dzonglha and Tsholo, past the Tsholo Tso, through a corridor of moraines and across braided glacial streams. Always by a most economical route, always direct, until just after

Phulung Karpo, when we realized we were almost at the hospital door, they disappeared. Later, when we were talking to Sirdar Ila Taschi about the tracks, he casually said, 'It was the wolf,' going on to explain that the Sherpa call the Chhugjuma Pass south of the Thso La the 'Pass of the Wolf', and that wolves have often been seen going between the two valleys.

Suffice to say, our celebrations were unreserved but by the time we descended to Namche Bazar, passing the heavily-laden yaks on Mendelphu Hill, our heads were as clear as the cold morning air.

ITINERARY:

The route we followed on the expedition went round the Khumbu in a roundabout way. The itinerary described below is more logical.

Note that by choosing the traditional Everest Expedition Route, rather than flying to Lukhla, an extra two weeks can be added to the trek in the following way:

DAY 1: KATHMANDU TO CHAUBAS (1,403m/4,600ft)
Drive to Dolalghat to begin trek. Long climb with distant views of Jugal Himal. Camp 6 – 7 hours.

DAY 2: CHAUBAS TO RISINGO (1,656m/5,430ft)
A good day's ridge walking with views of Jugal/Chetris/Brahmins. 5 – 6 hours.

DAY 3: RISINGO TO CHITRE (1,824m/5,980ft)
A day of many ups and downs. Good views of distant Himal. About 6 hours.

DAY 4: CHITRE TO KIRANTICHAP (1,092m/3,580ft)
Good views of Rolwaling Himal dominated by Gauri Shankar and Menlungtse/Manga Deorali (2,377m/7,797ft). First of seven passes *en route* to Khumbu. 5 – 6 hours.

DAY 5: KIRANTICHAP TO YARSA (1,708m/5,600ft)
Long descent to Bhote Khosi then ascends through forest and villages. 5 – 6 hours.

DAY 6: YARSA TO THOSE (1,482m/4,860ft)
A climb to the Chisapani Pass (2,500m/8,202ft) and a steep descent to the Sikri Khola then another pass to Those/Iron ore mining/chain link bridge building. 6 hours.

DAY 7: THOSE TO BHANDAR (1,738m/5,700ft)
Along river to Shivalaya, followed by steep climb, then more gradual to Chyangma Pass (2,705m/8,875ft), Sherpa country. Optional route to Thodung to visit cheese factory and *gompa*. Jiri 2 hours up Sikri Khola to the north. 7 hours. Those bussing to Jiri can join the trek here.

DAY 8: BHANDAR TO SETE (2,575m/8,450ft)
Descend to Phedi, cross bridge or follow river to Kenja. Then steep climb through forest to hill-top *gompa*. 5 hours.

DAY 9: SETE TO JUNBESI (2675m/8,775ft)
Long uphill to Lamjura Pass (3,530m/11,582ft). Rhododendrons and Rolwaling. Entry into Solu/Khumbu. Descent to Tragdobuck passing *mani*-walls, then traverse on north side of valley. Descend to medieval town with monastery. 6 – 7 hours.

DAY 10: JUNBESI TO TRAKSHINDU (3,071m/10,075ft)
Traverse the Solung ridge, where there is splendid walking and Everest views, Numbur and Karyolung. Ascend from Ringmo to Trakshindu Pass. Descent to *gompa*. 6 hours.

DAY 11: TRAKSHINDU TO KHARIKHOLA (2,004m/6,575ft)

Long descent to Dudh Khosi, and then ascent to Rai village, Jubing. Ascend through bamboo to Sherpa and Magyar bazaar. 6 hours.

DAY 12: KHARIKHOLA TO PUIYAN (2418m/7,930ft)

Plenty of ascents and descents high above the river. 6 hours.

DAY 13: PUIYAN TO MONJO (2,835m/9,300ft)

Stay on east side, meet Lukhla trail at Chaurikharka, cross rickety bridge at Phakding and follow west bank to Benkar. Cross to east bank, see Japanese lodge at Chumoa. Park entrance at Monjo.

Those flying to Lukhla join the trek at this point:

DAYS 1 – 2: KATHMANDU TO NAMCHE BAZAR

Morning flight to Lukhla, walk to Monjo, then camp or lodge.

DAYS 3 – 4: ACCLIMATIZATION

An enjoyable side trip from Namche goes west up the Bhote Khosi to Thami, a most interesting Sherpa village on the traditional route to Tibet over the Nagpa La. Thami was also the birthplace of Tensing Norgay. You can return the following day to Khumjung or Phortse.

DAY 15: NAMCHE TO PHORTSE (3,840m/12,598ft)

Via Kunde/Khumjung, beneath Khumbu Yul Lha, the sacred mountain of the Sherpas.

DAY 16: PHORTSE TO GOKYO (4,750m/15,584ft)

This is a long day, and there are many campsites. Follow on either left or right bank of river to Machhermo. Camp or use small lodges at Gokyo.

A day's exploration is worthwhile and advisable at Gokyo before crossing the Tsho La. A fast, fit party travelling light could go from Gokyo to Dzonglha in a day. The following is more normal:

DAY 17: GOKYO TO DRAGNAG (4,690m/15,387ft)

This is an easy day, crossing Ngozumpa snout. It is possible to combine this with a dawn ascent of Gokyo Ri. Camp.

DAY 18: DRAGNAG TO DZONGLHA (4,843m/15,889ft)

Cross Tsho La (5,420m/17,782ft) to Yersa. Stunning mountain views. Camp. 6 – 8 hours.

DAY 19: DZONGLHA TO LOBUJE (4,930m/16,175ft)

Descend to Tshola Tsho into Khumbu Valley, Duglha. Ascend to Lobuje. 5 – 6 hours.

DAY 20: LOBUJE TO KALA PATTAR (5,545m/18,192ft)

Ascend moraine, follow valley to Gorak Shep, and ascend Kala Pattar. Return to Lobuje.

Much more worthwhile is a camp at Gorak Shep. Ask at Lobuje about accommodation to give you time to enjoy this fantastic spot.

DAY 21: LOBUJE TO DINGBOCHE (4,542m/14,900ft)

Descend this classic valley to Pheriche. Cross moraine to Imja Valley and *yersa*, magnificent views. 6 hours.

DAY 22: DINGBOCHE TO THYANGBOCHE (3,867m/12,687ft)

Descend to Orsho and Pangboche. Cross bridge to *gompa*. 5 hours.

DAY 23: THYANGBOCHE TO NAMCHE

Descend to Phunki. Ascend to Trashinga and Sanasa. Open walking, stunning views. 5 hours.

DAY 24: NAMCHE TO LUKLHA (2,743m/9,000ft)

Descend, returning to Chaurikharka, and ascend to airstrip. 6 – 8 hours.

The author on steep ground above the South Face buttresses during the first ascent of Cholatse. (Photo: Vernon Clevinger.)

Many of the stages, especially in the early days, are very comfortable, with time for photography, visiting villages and enjoying the views.

DIFFICULTY:

The normal Everest Trek is strenuous but not technically difficult, involving straightforward hiking along good paths. However, there are many long ascents and descents and if the Tsho La is crossed, you will be on ice and snow (although this doesn't require specialist equipment). Good acclimatization is essential

for the safe ascent of high points such as Gokyo Ri and Kala Pattar. Those flying into Lukhla should take time to acclimatize around Namche.

LOGISTICS:

Flying in and out of Lukhla is the easiest approach, although poor weather and lack of flights can cause major headaches getting out again. Most people walking in favour the shorter approach from Jiri now that the road has been extended (it is not as good as the Expedition Route). Porters can become scarce and expensive in Lukhla, and yaks are a good alternative, but not for crossing the pass. All of this trek can be done using local lodges, of which there are many. The trek is within the Sagamartha National Park so that, apart from a trekking permit, you will need to pay an entry free of 250 NRPs at Jorsale Gate. Trekking parties camping in the park will also be required to carry paraffin (kerosene), as wood burning is not allowed.

EQUIPMENT:

Take normal trekking equipment. The Khumbu is high, so warm clothing is a must — a down vest or parka is a great comfort in the mornings and evenings. An ice-axe and short climbing rope can be useful on the pass in icy conditions.

MAPS:

The Mandala Trekking Maps provide good general trekking coverage and are adequate for most needs. The Schneider 1:50,000 Khumbu Himal sheet is far more detailed and accurate about the Khumbu area north of Namche Bazar. For the Everest area north of Pangboche the new *National Geographic* magazine's 1:50,000 sheet, produced by Brad Washburn, is superb. It includes the Tibetan side of Everest and gives a very clear overall picture of the mountain.

Abode of Snakes, Temples and Kings:
The Valley of Kathmandu

There are nearly as many temples as houses, and as many idols as inhabitants, there not being a fountain, a river or a hill within its limits that is not consecrated to one or other of the Hindu or Buddhist deities.

W. Kirkpatrick
An Account of the Kingdom of Nepaul, 1811

Had I bothered to log all the hours and days I've spent walking in and around the valley of Kathmandu it would be the longest trek I've ever made. But the addition has never been done and the journey has accumulated over many years, a little at a time, just enough before the senses were stunned by the wonder of it all. I can't imagine growing tired of it. For me, as with Dr Johnson and London, 'those who are tired of Kathmandu and its valley must be tired of life'.

Always on my return to Nepal there are days at the beginning and end of expeditions that have to be spent in Kathmandu. Sometimes those days seem quite hectic — an endless paper chase between ministries, searching for signatures that open doors to long-awaited adventures. At other times it's by taxi to Asan Tole, a crowded commercial quarter between the Rani Pokhari and Indra Chowk, to rummage for aluminium cooking pots, and the assorted paraphernalia of an expedition kitchen, in tiny open-fronted shops as carefully carved as the temples themselves. Or rushing to the 'Fresh House' off the New Road to buy food — 'dotting the i's and crossing the t's' before the off into the hills. But when the inevitable chores are completed I always find time for the valley. Sometimes it's just an hour or two wandering the back streets of Thamel, looking in book stores or buying curios, or walking after dark through the medieval Durbar Square, savouring the bustling sounds, sights and smells around the ancient wooden Kasthamandap Temple from which Kathmandu takes its name. The cacophony of temple bells, honking horns, barking dogs and ethnic diversity becomes a wondrous accompaniment to my magical mystery tours around the intricately-carved treasures of the city. Caught in a time warp, I like to wander down side streets to the past.

Sometimes, with days to spare, the terraced farmland and red brick villages beyond the dusty and increasingly hectic capital call. Villages like Thimi, a few kilometres east of the city across the Manohara Khola on the road to Bhaktapur, are architectural gems — a maze of narrow streets flanked by tall red-brick houses, shaded by overhanging eaves supported by intricately-carved struts. This decorative detail of traditional Newari carving is echoed in glorious window frames, often ravaged by age. Nearby Bhaktapur is a treasure of such carving and thankfully is being preserved with the help of UNESCO and the efforts of men like John

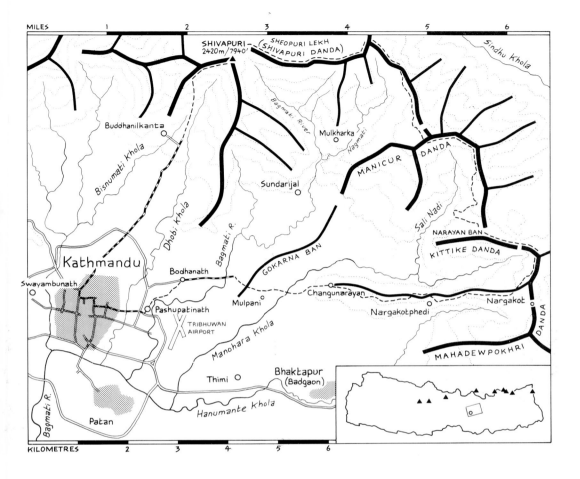

Sanday, who have also done much to conserve the treasures of Kathmandu's Durbar Square. Because of the nearness of clay from the Hanumante and Manohara rivers, Thimi has become a pottery centre. In the streets outside the crumbling brick houses, clay pots are thrown on simple wheels. The ochre-coloured wares are baked unglazed in the sun or in a kiln. They line the pavements alongside the narrow streets, stacked like the treasures from an archaeological dig: flower pots, water jugs, candle holders and jardiniéres in the form of mythological beasts. Elsewhere in the valley there are other knots of craftsmen where brassware, baskets, carpets and the traditional everyday essentials, not found in plastic, are still hand-made.

Returning to Kathmandu from a leisurely trek, it's easy to fall back into Western ways, jumping fast taxis and joining the round of the usual haunts. But the valley and its four cities, like the rest of Nepal, are best explored on foot. A bicycle, cheaply hired, is a close alternative if you want to cross the sacred Bagmati and Manohara rivers to visit the more distant cities of Kirtipur, Patan (Lalitpur), and Bhaktapur (Bhadgaon). These, with Kathmandu, were the centres of four Malla kingdoms, subdued and united by the Gurkha armies led by Prithinarayan Shah in 1767. Despite the passage of time the palaces and temples within their Durbars are essentially unchanged.

Returning from an expedition a few years ago,

At dawn on the rim of the Kathmandu Valley near Nargakot, looking across the cloud-filled Helmu district to the distant Himalaya.

I had several days free before my flight to Delhi. On past expeditions I have taken friends and clients to Nargakot on the Mahadewpokhri Danda, east of the city — always before dawn — to witness the sunrise on the Himalaya. On treks to Helambu, Langtang and Ganesh I've often climbed out of the valley on the walk north, enjoying the fantastic views that its ridge-line rim offers. So with days to spare I left the Kathmandu Guest House before dawn to hike the north rim of the valley from Nargakot to Shivapuri.

Walking out of town past Nag Pokhari and the Dhobi Khola, sharing the road with porters, I took only a light sleeping bag, some trail food — dried fruits, some nuts, the inevitable Nepali glucose biscuits — and a water bottle. Muscular porters strained behind large-wheeled carts pushing vast loads, their calves bulging with toil, while thin Newari porters moved loads suspended from a flexible pole carried yoke-like across a shoulder. They hurried past, their bobbing walk synchronized with the bouncing pole. By the time the sun had burned the mist from the sacred Bagmati River I had turned northwards along its west bank, to walk through riverside temples below the burning *ghats* of Pashupatinath. A few pencils of charcoal mixed with rice and orange flowers were all that remained of another mortal's final journey at the water's edge.

The temple, especially sacred to Hindus, is named after the Lord of Animals, Shiva. Although only Hindus can enter the main building, housing a huge image of a bull, others can wander amongst the myriad smaller shrines and lingum symbols on both sides of the river. In the sacred waters, which drain into the Ganga, *sardhus* (holymen) were bathing, whilst another group boiled rice and incanted mantras amongst the lingum on the far bank under the longing gaze of monkeys. It is not my favourite temple, but it does have a powerful, mystical quality, which later in the day would be spoilt when hoards of trippers, pilgrims and traders shatter its serenity.

Staying off the road, I had trouble finding a way through the jumble of houses northwards towards Bodhanath. By asking directions I soon had a companion who walked through fields with me to this massive *stupa*, reputed to be nearly 500 years old and containing the relics of Kashyapa Buddha. Centred in a massive square, its great dome was freshly painted white and stained with saffron. Above the dome, the all-seeing eyes look from a golden face through lines of fluttering prayer flags. Boddha is a favourite place. I like to wander round the square listening to the spinning prayer wheels and the chanted mantras of the Bhote people. Like a small Tibetan enclave it houses Buddhist monks and nuns, traders, and pilgrims who have also made the trek across the mountains. I had breakfast at Bodhanath, tea and biscuits in a *bhatti* on the main street; not stopping long, I wandered along the road eastwards towards Gorkana Ban, a route I have cycled many times.

Several years ago Changunarayan had been introduced to me by Lisa Van Gruisan Choegyal as having the most wonderful and ancient carvings in the valley. If you approach it from Gorkana, its glistening rooftop is clearly visible across the wide flood plain of the Manohara River, a hill-top temple at the end of a ridge leading towards Nargakot. I couldn't find a bridge beyond Mulpani, so instead I waded the shallow water and then climbed steeply to the pagoda-roofed temple to Vishnu guarded by Garuda, his winged messenger and mount. The oldest carvings, including an inscription said to date from the fifth century, are some of the most important in the valley.

I bivouacked exhausted after a long day on the Kittike Danda north of Nargakot, falling asleep in my down bag watching the sunset burnish the peaks towards Everest. Armed as I was with iodine crystals, drinking water presented no problem but I was gasping for a brew of tea and

An intricately-carved Newari door, common throughout the Kathmandu Valley.

reminded myself to bring a stove — next time. I could have wandered back towards Nargakot where there are several lodges providing tourist facilities, but I was enjoying the solitude and was too tired to make the effort.

November nights can be cold; this one was. The sky had been clear, my sleeping bag too thin and the lack of a Karrimat Foam stupid. Between bouts of shivering with clenched teeth, I was able to appreciate the brilliance of the night and the heavens crowded with stars. Sleeping not far from the path I was discovered by two lightly-clothed boys amused at my sleeping bag photography. They stayed long enough to enjoy the stunning sunrise, before

hurrying on towards the roadhead where the tourist buses would be gathering and I suppose an income was to be had as 'guides'. Soon warmed by the sun, I watched the light gradually fill the deep valley to the north, catching the contours of the terraces to create a geographer's relief model.

Armed with a poor map I had trouble finding a good route, but since getting lost here is of little consequence I took the line of least resistance, and descended too far into the drainage system of the Sali Nadi down the flank of the Narayan Ban, before stumbling on a path and people who directed me northwards. I climbed through numerous small settlements opting for a westward-leading path along a ridge marking the watershed between the Manohara and the Indrawati rivers. Eventually it wound a way through scrubby pastures and forest thick with rhododendrons along the Manichur Danda to Burlang Bhanjyang (2,438m/8,000ft), at a junction with the path leading north into Helambu and Gosainkund. I had been here before, and knew full well that the road south led to Sundarijal and 'civilization' as others know it. Instead, I opted to descend to the tiny settlement of Chaubas (2,233m/7,525ft), a Tamang village below the pass where I slept the night and bought hot food from a friendly family. No varied menu here, just the traditional Nepali staple of *dhalbhaat* and delicious vegetable stew. When I first came to Nepal this was the usual fare in *bhattis* everywhere. Unfortunately, demand from tourists has resulted in more complicated menus being offered; cooking these menus has un-doubtedly increased the problem of deforest-ation in areas where tourists congregate.

In the morning I regained the *bhanjyang* and followed the crest of the Shivapuri Danda, enjoying the views and life on the move. Fit after being 'high' for a long time, it's surprising how much ground can be covered when you are alone. A good track led at last to Shivapuri

Caught in a time warp — wandering back streets into the past.

Buddhanilkanta, where an eleventh century statue of a reclining Vishnu sleeps on a bed of snakes, upon whom the Kings of Nepal must never gaze.

(2,420m/7,940ft), which, although less than 9km (6 miles) from Kathmandu, is worlds apart and is also the highest point on the valley rim. At one time a religious teacher, Shivapuri Baba lived here and his ruined hut can be found close by. The forests around Shivapuri are protected and in the springtime the flowering rhododendrons must be spectacular. I descended almost jogging to the forest gate, joining the road to Buddhanilakantha and the shrine of the Vishnu asleep on a bed of snakes. This impressive carving is said to be over 900 years old.

Back in Kathmandu there is much for the visitor to see. A rapid tour of the four cities and the major temples will have you going back for a much more leisurely pilgrimage. Trying to take the whole lot in will simply lead to sensory overload, and see you back at your hotel in a state of culture shock pleading for mercy. Bauddha, Pashupati and Swayambu should be high on your list but need time to be absorbed. I find it's not enough simply to look at the buildings, guidebook in hand, trying to make sense of the iconography, which throughout Nepal seems utterly confused. The temples, although ancient, are not museums and I find it much more satisfying to step back as it were and absorb the pious Nepali people for whom the gods and these buildings are a part of everyday life. Take Swayambunath, for example. It can be seen, to the west of the city, across the Vishnumati River crowning an island-like hill rising from the flat bed of the valley. Looking out across the boundary walls of the main *stupa*, thought to be the oldest in the valley, you get spectacular views of Kathmandu and the distant, snow-covered Himal. It's possible to take a taxi to the southern end of the temple complex and climb up an easy incline to the top, but to really appreciate the scale of things, walk to Swayambu from the Durbar Square along Pie Alley, which leads eventually across the river. The base of Swayambu hill is guarded by a high prayer wall breached by an arched gate. Outside

the gate, a huge *mani*-wheel housed in a simple room is turned by devout locals going about their daily chores.

Inside the gate a wide paved path leads past peaceful Buddhas seated in a tranquil wood. Listen to the birdsong and monkey chatter mix with the sound of temple bells and horns as you walk beneath shady trees. But these are soon lost in the mantra of your own breathing as you climb the final step stone stairway to the summit.

The impressive *stupa* is centred in a square packed with smaller temples, bells and a formidable *dorje* (thunderbolt), a wonderful place that throngs with worshippers who share their offerings with the gods and troops of boisterous monkeys. Beyond the *stupa* is a *gompa* housing a brilliant Buddha, beyond which, from a dark interior, resonates the deep mantra of the monks.

A hawker selling suntala *on the street in Durbar Square, protected by mythological beasts.*

Seen from the hill the morphology of the valley in reality is well explained in myth. Legend has it that the valley was once filled by a lake (it was), and the waters were the home of great snakes, which wreathed and swam amongst the lotus, and gave the place its ancient name – Nag-hrad, or 'abode of snakes'. From the lake a heavenly lotus rose above all others; the embodiment of divine nature. From the north a demi-god Manjushri, with his followers, visited Nag-hrad to worship the manifestation.

Realizing that this was a godly place, he slashed at the bank with his sword (Chobar Gorge) to drain the lake from the valley. After this the lotus turned to stone, forming the hill on which Swayambunath stands, and Manjushri and his followers inhabited the valley. Throughout Nepal, reality wrapped in legend provides acceptable explanations to creation and, for most Nepalese, the spiritual answers to existence.

ITINERARY:

DAY 1: KATHMANDU TO NARGAKOT

Most people taxi to Nargakot for sunrise. There are lodges to stay overnight.

DAY 2: NARGAKOT TO BURLANG BHANJYANG

Ridge-top walking, heavily wooded in places. Trails quite confusing. Overnight at Bhatti.

DAY 3: BURLANG BHANJYANG TO SHIVAPURI AND KATHMANDU

Continue along the valley rim to its high point. Wonderful woods and flowers in springtime. Descend through woods to Buddhanilkanta. Bus/taxi to Kathmandu.

You can also do this short trek in a traditional manner, taking along Sherpas, tents and a cook.

For visitors to Kathmandu there can be no set itinerary and no single visit can do it justice. With only a few days to spare the serious sightseer will want to visit all four cities: Kathmandu, Patan, Bhaktapur and Kirtipur. All have wonderful buildings, temples, carvings and squares, at one time fit for princes to live in.

As well as the cities there are numerous temples that are amongst the most important, including Bodhanath, Changunarayan,

Swayambunath, Pashupati and the sleeping Vishnu of Buddhanilkanta. Along the way it will be impossible not to see a thousand other temples and beautiful buildings.

If you have time, don't restrict yourself to cities and temples. There are many small villages close to Kathmandu where Newari farmers and craftsmen live, untouched by the city close at hand. Thimi is a particular favourite of mine, but there are many more.

If you haven't got time to walk around the valley rim, drive to Nargakot. Be there for sunrise or sunset. You can take a taxi there and could walk back through Changunarayan and Bodhanath.

DIFFICULTY:

All very simple, although I found the route-finding along the rim quite difficult in places. Water is scarce.

LOGISTICS:

Again, quite simple. I actually walked all of it, but you could take a taxi to Nargakot and back again at the end. You can also leave the ridge in several places, the most obvious of which is at the Burlang Bhanjyang to descend to

A woman near Swayambu cleans huge brass water containers with a mixture of mud and straw.

Sundarijal. Alternatively, you can treat each section as a separate day hike. Indeed, the hike to Shivapuri is one of the most popular in the valley. No trekking permit is required for this area.

SEASON:

This can be done at any time during the year. During the monsoon months there will be little to see, although the flowers and birds might be spectacular; the paths will be muddy and as slippery as hell.

MAP:

Kathmandu Valley. 1:50,000 Kartographische Anstalt Freytag-Berndt und Artaria.

In Tilman's Wake:
Through Langtang and Jugal

From my youth upwards my spirit walked with the souls of men ... my griefs, my passions and my powers made me a stranger ... my joy was in the wilderness.

Lord Byron

As September passes, the skies of Nepal become increasingly clear. The mountains, no longer threatened by the steamy heat from the Indian Plains, lose their menacing grey castles of cumulus full of monsoon rain, and float instead in a moat of infinite blue. It's then that the skyline north of Kathmandu stands out like the jaw of a great white shark, with row upon row of glistening teeth — 'fangs excrescent upon the jaws of the earth', as Mallory said.

Due north of Kathmandu, a little over thirty kilometres away, are the Himals of Langtang and Jugal, easily seen in the clear months from hotel rooftops and high points within the capital such as Swayambu. They form a beckoning backdrop beyond the valley rim. Separated from the Ganesh Himal in the west by the Bhote Khosi (a river from Tibet, itself a natural routeway through the mountains and at one time vitally important for trade with Kyirongdzong), the Langtang Valley extends eastwards from the Bhote Khosi, over-deepened by glaciers, and ends profoundly in a high mountain wall that is a natural boundary with Tibet. To the south-east the Jugal is defined by yet another Bhote River flowing south to join

the Sun Khosi. A recent reclassification of the area by Harka Gurung has defined the Langtang Himal as those mountains north of the Langtang Khola, and the Jugal as those to the south and south-east.

The nearness of Langtang Valley to Kathmandu and its proximity to the Tibetan border, coupled with the region's ruggedness, make it an attractive trekking proposition. This is especially the case for those on a tight schedule, since a road of sorts now extends to Dhunche from Trisuli Bazar up the valley of the Trisuli Gandaki, which beyond Syabrubensi becomes the Bhote Khosi. From the roadhead, which can be reached in six to eight hours from Kathmandu, Langtang Village can be trekked comfortably in three days along a route well served by lodges.

Paradoxically, the valleys and ridges that flow south from Langtang and Jugal offer some of the best undeveloped trekking in Nepal. The area provides an opportunity for the adventurous and self-contained party to follow in Tilman's wake and rediscover the high passes and pristine valleys he found in 1949.

On the recommendation of John Cleare, who had traversed the area with Ian Howell in 1976, I put together a trip that would take me through the Helambu District over the Ganja La into Langtang. From here, after some climbing, we would travel east up the valley to Langsisa Kharka, before returning south in an attempt to cross a higher glacier pass between Urkingmang

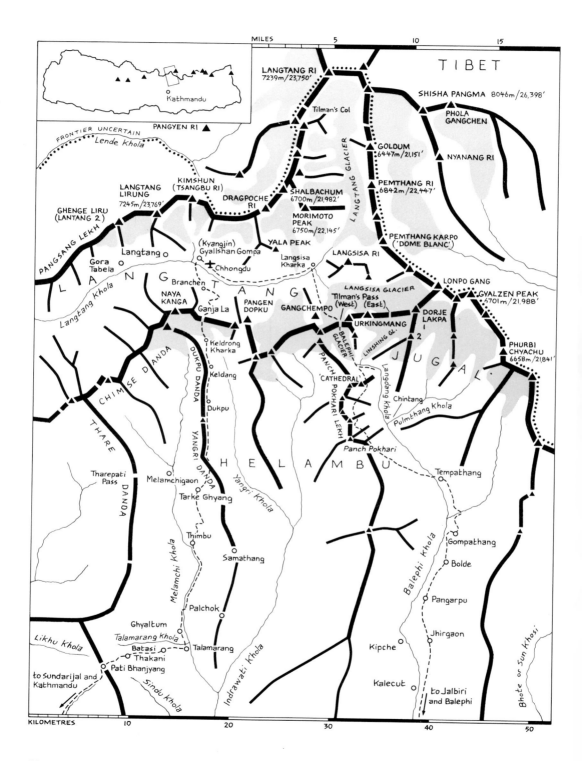

MILES

5   10   15

Kathmandu

TIBET

LANGTANG RI
7239m/23,750'

SHISHA PANGMA 8046m/26,398'

PHOLA GANGCHEN

Tilman's Col

PANGYEN RI ▲

FRONTIER UNCERTAIN
Lende Khola

GOLDUM
6447m/21,151'

NYANANG RI

PEMTHANG RI
6842m/22,447'

LANGTANG GLACIER

KIMSHUN
(TSANGBU RI)

LANGTANG LIRUNG
7245m/23,769'

DRAGPOCHE RI

SHALBACHUM
6700m/21,982'

GHENGE LIRU
(LANTANG 2)

MORIMOTO PEAK
6750m/22,145'

PEMTHANG KARPO
('DOME BLANC')

PANGSANG LEKH

Gora Tabela

Langtang ○

YALA PEAK

(Kyangjin)
Gyallshan Gompa

✛ Chhongdu

Langsisa Kharka

LANGSISA RI

LONPO GANG

GYALZEN PEAK
6701m/21,988'

L A N G Branchen

Langtang Khola

NAYA KANGA

Ganja La

T A N G

PANGEN DOPKU

GANGCHEMPO

Langsisa Kharka

LANGSISA GLACIER

Tilman's Pass
(West) (East)

URKINGMANG

1
2

DORJE LAKPA

PHURBI CHYACHU
6658m/21,841'

○ Keldrong Kharka

CHIMSE DANDA

DUKPU DANDA

BALEPHI GLACIER

PANCH POKHARI LEKH

LINSHING GL.

Langdang Khola

J U G A L

○ Keldang

'CATHEDRAL'

Chintang

THARE DANDA

○ Dukpu

YANGRI DANDA

Pulmthang Khola

Tharepati Pass

○ Melamchigaon

H E L A M B U

Panch Pokhari

Tempathang

DANDA

○ Tarke Ghyang

Yangri Khola

Gompathang

○ Thimbu

○ Bolde

○ Samathang

Melamchi Khola

Balephi Khola

Pangarpu

Likhu Khola

○ Palchok

Jhirgaon

Ghyaltum
Talamarang Khola

○ Batasi
○ Thakani
Pati Bhanjyang

○ Talamarang

Indrawati Khola

Kipche

Bhote or Sun Khosi

to Sundarijal and
Kathmandu

Sindu Khola

Kalecut ○

to Jalbiri
and Balephi

KILOMETRES

10   20   30   40   50

and Gangchempo. This in turn would enable us to reach the headwaters of the Balephi Khola and so return south to the Sun Khosi west of Lamasangu.

My group, an assortment of trekkers and mountaineers, had been assembled from the United States and Britain by Mountain Travel for me to lead. At the time this was the only way I could finance the expedition. I was fortunate since, despite a long-held belief that the best way to travel in the mountains is either alone or with a local, and that the only way to climb is with a small party of close friends, we got on surprisingly well. They were good company and, by the time we were well on our way into Langtang, had formed a cohesive if diverse group. We included an emergency doctor and his wife with a shared enthusiasm for mountains and medicine. A computer programmer whose logical powers and intellect were as high as a Doric column; with the rest of us he shared a love of wild places and mountains in particular. From Colorado were two friends, both geologists with an interest in oil and mountaineering. Having 'cut their teeth' in Eldorado they wanted to hone their skills in the Himalaya. Finally, myself, a university teacher who had given up my post for higher things — mountains!

Beginning the trek towards the Sherpa settlements of Helambu couldn't be easier. We travelled by bus past the immense *stupa* of Bodhanath to Sundarijal where Gyalzen our Sirdar was assembling a hardy team of porters for the trek north. Knowing full well the difficult terrain ahead, and anticipating snow on the passes, perhaps lots of it, only hillmen, including a large number of Sherpas (both men and women), were selected as porters. As well as extra food we also brought from Kathmandu a full set of clothing for each of the porters, including extra socks, gloves and dark glasses. The result may have looked like Napoleon's forces retreating across Russia, or a sick parade of Fred Karno's army, but the effect on morale as each difficulty was met by a new kit issue was amazing.

The first days on trek are ones of adjustment — getting used to a new routine in hill time after the frenetic pace of life before departure and the uncivilized experience of long-haul air travel via Delhi. It takes time as well to adjust to the new physical strains of wearing a pack and hiking for most of the day, up hill and down, especially down, into very deep dales. Then, of course, there is the need to adjust to being part of a strange and dynamic social group. But what I at least never have trouble getting used to are the long nights of well-earned sleep.

From the roadhead the trail climbs towards the valley rim up a giant staircase through damp forest. Rusting pipes from a powerstation parallel the path, leaking pin-hole jets of water that become arcs of colour in the sun. Where the water gathers in pools or trickles down the red-brown pipes, vivid green algae and moss grow richly. Exodus from the valley takes about three hours, the time it take to top the Shivapuri Ridge just beyond Chaubas at Burlang Bhanjyang (2,438m/8,000ft). Ahead the not-so-distant Langtang and Jugal Himal are spectacular and beckoning, so, with the urgency for progress that Day One brings, we didn't linger long but descended from the pass through farmland to a saddle that marks the watershed between the headwaters of the Likhu and the Sindju Kholas. Astride the saddle is the settlement of Pati Bhanjyang where our trek permits were checked at a police post. This caused a mild bout of panic when it was found that a permit had been packed, and was somewhere ahead on the back of a porter. Fortunately he was quickly found and the pass was returned and duly displayed.

From the saddle the trail divides. Due north the route follows the Thare Danda towards the holy lakes of Gosainkund, whilst ours went north-east into the valley of the Talamarang Khola and the Sherpa enclaves within the

Trekking the Thare Danda near Pati Bhanjyang, looking across the hills and valleys of Helambu with the snow-capped Langtang and Jugal Himal beyond.

catchment of the Melamchi Khola. Had we had more days to spare we could have taken the northern route to Tharepati, where a high trail then traverses the head of the Melamchi, the Tamang/Sherpa villages of Melamchigaon, Takedau and Nakotegaon to Tarke Ghyang; undoubtedly a more scenic route.

Descending the southern flank of the Talamarang River on a rough path the route passes through Thakani and Batase before crossing the river to Talamarang Village (not marked on the new Schneider Helambu/ Langtang map) — after a knee-pounding 800-metre descent. Following a wide rough track the way now turns north into the Melamchi Valley, through scruffy villages along the west bank.

It took two long days to reach the 'temple of 100 horses', the prosperous Sherpa village of Tarke Ghyang. As the largest community in Helambu it is home for many Sherpas and Tamangs, with t-shops and accommodation for trekkers. The original *gompa* was built around

1727, but the present one dates from around 1969. When Tilman passed by on his way south he described the monastery as 'a building half corrugated iron and half picturesque decay'. Obviously repairs were underway then for he mentions the Lama supervising paintings by local artists, including a Wheel of Life and domestic scenes which he mentions as 'resolutely and offensively coarse'. They are still there!

Before leaving the Helambu to venture north towards the Ganja La, it's worth mentioning that the Sherpa of Helambu are quite distinct from those of the Solu/Khumbu. Although they appear similar physically, their language is different, as are their dress and customs. In particular the women traditionally wear red cotton dresses, instead of the dark wrap-around Ungi and Shyama, the striped woven apron typical of Khumbu Sherpanis.

Climbing past the *gompa* on a trail made difficult by landslides we gained the crest of the Yangri Danda, which was quite narrow in places. After crossing several notches in spurs dropping to the Yangri Khola, we traversed the eastern flank of the Dupku Danda, entering numerous cwms between the spurs on a hillside dotted with summer pastures. Once out of the Helambu there are no more lodges or permanent settlements until Langtang, so the capacity to be self-contained is essential. As with many high-level walks, water, or the lack of it, can be a problem. In the autumn months there was no water at Dupku Kharka (4,023m/13,200ft), but at the kharka beyond (a cwm facing east with a big boulder and smoke-blackened rock shelter on its northern flank) there is water a short distance below. Beyond Dupku, after a long day of undulating hiking, the traversing trail meets a broad flat valley below the Ganga La Glacier, beyond which Keldrong Kharka (4,298m/ 14,100ft) provides a superb campsite.

In all, it took three days from Tarke Ghyang to reach a campsite near a small glacial tarn on the southern side of the la. West of the pass is the attractive summit of Naya Kanga (5,846m/ 19,180ft), a delightful official 'trekking peak', normally climbed by its north-east ridge. However, this camp (4,877m/16,000ft) was a splendid base from which to explore the impressive glacial cwm and small peaks of what the Schneider map calls the Urking Kangari. A ridge-line beginning some distance up the glacier west of the Ganga La provided some good sport; it should have led to a point just west of the summit of Naya Kanga, but dangerous snow conditions put an end to our attempt.

Crossing a short section of easy glacier, we climbed without difficulty up some snow-covered rocks leading to the crest of the Ganja La. On the ridge a cairn of slates, sporting a crop of bamboo wands from which dropped tattered prayer flags, marked the crossing. Southwards, down the valley of the Yangri, the views were memorable, as interlocking spurs gave way to distant ridges and an infinite horizon; but northwards the view was unforgettable. Across

the valley the nearest peaks of the Langtang group, including Shalbachum (6,700m/ 21,982ft), soared above the flat-floored depths, east of which the Langtang Glacier was ringed by a wall of peaks that extended from Langsisa Ri (6,370m/20,898ft), through to Langtang Ri (7,239m/23,750ft); but over all and looking touchably close was the crenelated crest of Shishapangma (8,046m/26,398ft), wholly in Tibet, and the last 8,000-metre peak to be climbed.

Now we were to experience a common phenomenon on north-facing slopes of the Himalaya — unconsolidated depth hoar. The brilliant weather of the post-monsoon had been perfect, although the cold clear nights sent us early to our tents. However, as often happens in my experience, and in that of others if expedition accounts are to be believed, there were several brief periods of snowfall between the middle and the end of October. For normal trekking they would go unnoticed, eaten by the morning sun before you stopped for lunch, but up high on glaciers and passes things are different. Had it been spring, the consequences would have been negligible, for as the season moves towards summer the days grow warmer and the snow has a chance to melt and consolidate. However, in the autumn, with winter approaching, the days and nights grow colder and the snow stays as a bottomless powder.

Descending the sunless northern slope was difficult, as hand and footholds had to be excavated from beneath unsupporting powder that seeped into gloves and shirt-necks instantly. In the end we fixed a line down from the col for the porters' and our own safety. Then, in thigh-deep snow, we ploughed a trench down the moraine-covered hillside towards the valley. Following the line of least resistance was not as easy as it sounds. From time to time a bottomless pit between boulders left the leader chest-deep in snow, wallowing without support and unable to break free. Hollows provided problems too; filled in by wind-blown powder, their surfaces, although mill-pond flat, were a maelstrom for an un-suspecting mountaineer. Adopting the Sherpa norm of smiling in the face of adversity, we rolled around in bouts of rib-aching laughter, leaving the unfortunate victim to flail like an egg-beater trying to get free. By the time we reached the stone huts at Branchen, we were exhausted but happy.

Over the next few days we camped at Kyangjin Gompa near to the Government Cheese Factory, which provided as good a base as any from which to explore the area.

Porters, tough and cheerful like this Tamang, are the 'Pickfords' of the Himalayas.

The Langtang Valley was created a National Park in 1976 and remains the second largest in Nepal, covering an area of nearly 1,700 square kilometres (660 square miles). Within its boundaries are forty-five villages and numerous summer settlements used for trans-humance farming during the monsoon. These are home to a people not unlike the Sherpa, who are thought to have come from near Kyirongdzong in Tibet. Their language, on the other hand, is said to resemble that of the Tibetans of Sikkim.

The Langtang below Gora Tabela is still heavily wooded with blue pine, oak, birch and bamboo. In springtime these hillsides are a riot of colourful rhododendrons. This verdant forest provides an ideal habitat for Nepal's elusive wildlife — 'elusive' because, although the park is the recorded home of more than one thousand plants, one hundred and sixty bird species and thirty mammals (including serow, goral and the rare red panda), the majority have eluded me and my camera on numerous visits.

Beyond Gora Tabela and the tree-line the valley has a classical 'U'-shaped profile, formed by the now retreating Langtang Glacier. Contained between the Pangsang Lekh to the north and the Chimsedang Lekh to the south the valley is comparable to the Lauterbrunnen in Switzerland or Yosemite in California. Although there are none of Nepal's 8,000-metre giants, the surrounding Himals contain a plethora of impressive peaks, including Langtang Lirung (Gangchen Ledrub) (7,245m/ 23,769ft), which rises sharply to the north above Langtang village.

This village and its inhabitants retained much that is Tibetan. Many of the older men were wearing long coats or *chuba* in the style of Sherpas, and skin jackets with the fleece on the inside. Long hair worn in braids was also common, as were knee-length boots with a heavy hide sole and woollen embroidered uppers. Unlike the Sherpa of Khumbu, how-ever, the Langtangba were not a particularly welcoming bunch and I, for one, was glad to be going high again.

North and east of Kyangjin is a confused area of snaking moraines whose high points are marked by bamboo wands and prayer flags. Despite the amount of snow covering them, these mounds of rubbished mountains provided highways into a desolate glacier wastescape. The nearest high point, which we called Kyangjin Ri (4,773m/15,659ft), was a splendid place from which to study the area's geography.

Closest at hand, at the head of a tortured mass of tumbling glacier to the north-west, is the 'monarch of the glen', Langtang Lirung. Extending eastwards in a barrier of rock and ice are a line of peaks that includes Kimshun (6,745m/22,129ft), Dragpoche Ri (6,543m/ 21,466ft) and Shalbachum (6,918m/22,696ft). According to the Mandala maps this forms the frontier with Tibet. Sandwiched between Shalbachum and Morimoto Peak, a cluster of smaller peaks looked perfect for our needs.

From the same viewpoint looking east was a mountain which was obviously not high but was set apart by both its position and fascia of folded ice; its shadows looked as though they had been drawn in soft pencil on white paper. Its ethereal form, all light and shade, changed throughout the day, but at sunset its shadows deepened to purple, off-setting the sun-caught, blood-red highlights of its curtain-fold flanks. Unimaginatively called 'Fluted Peak' by Tilman, perhaps in keeping with the scientific nature of his quest, the mountain is better named Gangchempo (6,387m/20,955ft), and, alas, not on any permitted climbing list, although its altitude would make it a perfect 'trekking peak'. Officially still awaiting an ascent, it has in fact been the target of several unofficial ones.

Leaving our base at the *gompa* we placed a high camp in a snow-covered pasture above the *yersa* of Yala, which we reached by traversing the steep hillside and moraines on the north side of the valley above the STOL airstrip at Chhongdu. Between the stone huts of Tharche Pisa and Thikyapsa we flushed a large herd of *tahr*, a goat-like antelope, which continued ahead of us, contouring and grazing the snow-covered hillside.

From our camp it was a short distance to the sharp edge of a stepped glacier which, after some obvious crevasses had been avoided, led via a well-defined snow ridge to an attractive summit, possibly Yala Peak (5,500m/18,045ft). This is a climb that is Alpine in character, with a panorama that is truly Himalayan. Some confusion exists over names and indeed the detail of the area, since both the Mandala Trekking and the Schneider maps have major inaccuracies. Descending from High Camp to Base it snowed, which didn't augur well for plans to explore the upper valley and to cross yet another high pass.

Meanwhile, back at the monastery another party had camped, the only other Westerners we saw on the whole trip. They were a welcome diversion, having just returned from Langsisa Kharka from where they had tried to cross Tilman's Pass to the Balephi. Their Sirdar was a distant cousin of Gyalzen, our Sirdar — since Khumbu Sherpas number only three and a half thousand, being related is no difficult thing! They were despondent over their failure, so I helped them devour some potted delicacies they were carrying for just such an occasion. The whole was washed down with the best local *rakshi*, and I remember it as a wonderfully warm evening, despite the hard frost. Between spoonfuls of garlic-cloves in honey and pickled stem ginger, transported from Hong Kong, I interrogated them about the route. As we had discovered on the Ganja La, waist-deep snow now awaited us on the approach to Tilman's. Having dined well but not wisely, I walked back to my tent with all the deliberation that *rakshi* and altitude necessitate!

During a night disturbed by thoughts and heartburn, my best plans were laid.

Amongst the ice near Tsergo Ri with Gangchempo (6,387m/20,955ft), Tilman's 'Fluted Peak' beyond.

It was vital that we travel light, relieved of everything not essential to survival. From personal luggage went spare clothes, some of which were distributed amongst the Sherpa porters who would make the crossing. From the kitchen went all food luxuries — well, almost all — and in their place went high-calorie staples that would feed us all. The lightweight cane camp stools which I always take on a long trip made a marvellous camp fire (before the pass), much appreciated by our porters. Our excess was returned to Kathmandu with Gyalzen's cousin, whilst we continued eastwards along the valley floor, past the airstrip and several summer settlements to a solitary and desolate stone hut set in the snow-covered Langsisa Kharka (4,084m/13,399ft).

Ahead, the Langtang Glacier valley curved northwards beneath an unbreached barrier of peaks forming the border with Tibet. Beginning with Langsisa Ri (6,400m/20,997ft), it includes Pemthang Karpo (6,830m/22,408ft), Pemthang Ri (6,842m/22,447ft) and Goldum (6,447m/21,151ft), after which there is an unseen col, discovered by Toni Hagen whose extensive explorations followed Tilman's in the 1950s. At the head of the valley is Langtang Ri. The true right bank of the glacier is contained by an equally impressive mountain wall that ends in Morimoto Peak (6,750m/22,146ft). Tilman's maps, seemingly a joint effort between him and Lloyd, are appalling, but show three cols, one of which is on the actual Ganges/Tsangpo divide.

In the light of snow conditions the decision was made to cut short out explorations north, and instead concentrate on the col leading south through the Jugal.

From Langsisi, between the peaks of Gangchempo and Langsisa Ri, a narrow ice-formed trough, cut by the Langsisa Glacier, curves eastwards behind Langsisa Ri. It fills another amphitheatre of peaks, including Lenpo Gang (7,083m/23,238ft), the striking form of Dorje Lakpa (6,990m/22,993ft) and Urkinmang (6,151m/20,180ft), the cream (with the exception of Phurbi Chyachu (6,658m/21,841ft)) of the Jugal Himal.

Soon after sunrise, following an intensely cold night, our reduced team crossed a web of shallow glacier streams, careful of the ice-glazed boulders and rocks used as stepping-stones. Following a track made unburdened the day before, we continued along the crest of a long lateral moraine beneath the east wall of Gangchempo. Blown by the morning wind and caught by the sun, snow crystals danced in the air beneath a blue-black sky, whilst porters moved along the moraine crest, silhouetted against glistening ice. Walking along the ridge proved easier than the descent from the Ganja La, so we made camp in reasonable time. Our tents were perched amongst boulders on the moraine, with the Langsisa Glacier stretching away eastwards below the ramparts of Dorje Lakpa. We had found a level place amongst a nightmare of moraines where a secondary glacier descended from a low point in the ridge, between Urkinmang and another summit that in turn connected with Gangchempo. It would appear that Tilman's Col marks the lowest point on this ridge, although from the badly-drawn maps it could possibly be further east. With loaded porters that looked hopeless, whereas ours merely seemed impossible!

As the sky darkened and the sun set, the ridges in front of our camp were thrown into deep shadow, whilst the high peaks beyond retained the light. Rising from the glacier towards Urkinmang was a curving ridge with two upstanding rock pinnacles sharply defined against the still-glistening Dorje Lakpa. These towers are said by locals to be the petrified images of the Buddhist saints Guru Rimpoche and Shakya Muni.

Not getting up until the sun warms the tent is not only sensible but essential, otherwise the rime that forms inside begins to melt and everything is soaked. Leaving the sleeping bags to air and the porters to rest or descend for wood, we carried on trail-breaking towards the col. Often in wasit-deep snow, we ploughed our furrow over moraines to gain a point on the glacier west of the col which was revealed as a narrow cleft. Unable to rally the enthusiasm for a final bout of 'dog-paddle' in the full heat of the day, we turned tail and headed for home.

The benefits of trail-breaking the day before became obvious and seemed worthwhile as we gained the crest of Tilman's Col (5,304m/ 17,400ft) in good time. In a snowy hollow beneath the west flank of Urkinmang we were amazed to find a cache of equipment. Not the sort of cache left for future use, but rather equipment jettisoned in haste, including clothing, food and cooking pots.

Load carrying up the moraines that lead to Tilman's Pass below the tumbling hanging glaciers on Urkingmang (6,150m/20,180ft)

Southwards the Balephi Glacier fell away in steepening convex slopes hiding from us the icefall below. Forewarned by Cleare about this difficulty, we moved over to the left side of the glacier close to the rocks or Urkinmang. The snow, less deep on the southern side, nevertheless still presents difficulties as it covers hard glacier ice beneath. Between the ice and some rock terraces further to the left is an awkward step over soft snow and slabs which was easily overcome with a fixed rope which enabled the porters nimbly to gain the terraces and traverse to the top of a large snow-covered scree chute. With all apparent difficulty behind us, and the sight of meadows below, the whole party quickly slid and glissaded to a camp by a frozen moraine pond. Surrounded by attractive rock peaks, the small cwm beneath the col soon lost the sun to become an ice-box and sent everybody scurrying to their tents. Sherpas and porters looked as though they were performing a university rag stunt as they piled endless numbers into what formerly had been two-man tents. For those with the dubious fortune of being in the middle, it must have felt like a sub-tropical hell!

Keeping to the east lateral moraine of the glacier, we descended beneath what Cleare and Howell called Freney Peak to a meadow near the confluence of the Balephi and Linshing Glacier, finding *en route* a new 100 metre rope and a new pair of double boots. Although we were still high, and there was a considerable amount of snow about, there was plenty of scrub rhododendron for porter fires. Revelling in the relative luxury of this camp which caught the early-morning sun after it rose over the shoulder of Phurbi Chyachu (6,658m/21,844ft), we were now faced with a dilemma. We had either to attempt to follow the Balephi Khola through its entire course, which was unknown to us and our Sirdar, or follow a high-level path along the eastern flank of the Panch Pokhari Lekh, which we knew existed but which was obviously going to be under snow.

In the end we agreed on a compromise. Two Sherpas and I would descend the river, called at this point (on the Schneider Map) the 'Lagdang Khola', eastwards to a place where it obviously entered a narrow gorge. If a trail existed, and the way ahead was possible for loaded porters, we would light a fire as a signal for them to descend. If, on the other hand, the fire hadn't been lit by midday they were to cross the first of many small 'cols' on the traverse, and camp in the first cwm or suitable hollow they found; we would catch up later.

In the event the descent began well. We discovered a faint track which contoured above the river, and seemed to be heading towards the top of the narrow rocky cleft marking where the river turned southwards. However, it soon faded, and we were forced to descend a steep hillside of boulders and scrub rhododendron with increasing difficulty. The gorge was also beginning to look less appealing; its glistening rocks which, from above, we had taken to be mica-schist were in fact ice-glazed, offering no safe descent for porters.

Late that afternoon we caught the main party up after regaining several thousand lost feet. Slowed by yet more deep snow on the north-facing side of the hill, they were trying to gain a cairned notch on a spur thrown down towards the east from an attractive rock peak. In different conditions this would provide splendid walking, but under deep soft snow it was hard work to find good footing on the boulder-strewn hillside. Once at the notch the view southwards down the valley was magnificent — an endless vista of interlocking spurs and blue receding horizons. Camp once again was cold comfort, but the position more than made up for it. From this high hollow we could look out over the southern and western walls of Dorje Lakpa II (6,523m/21,400ft), Gyalzen Peak (6,701m/ 21,988ft) and of course the unmistakable Phurbi Chyachu.

The trekking, despite the cold and difficult conditions, was magnificent, following as it did an occasional traceable trail across a precipitous hillside which threw down long spurs, like the flying buttresses of a massive cathedral. Between each of these ramparts the hillside dished into boulder- and scrub-filled hollows, which obviously provided good grazing in other seasons. Our porters made use of the plentiful dried yak pies they found around for fuel.

Below, the hillside fell steeply away through dense forest to an unseen river far below. On the far side of the main valley a tributary, the Pulmthang Khola, rising on the flanks of Phurbi Chyachu, had cut its own impressive course, below which we could see that the Balephi valley was no longer a profound gorge. From my

A wooden suspension bridge across the Langtang Khola below the Ganja La.

research I knew that this junction of the Pulmthang and Langdang rivers was where the Scottish Ladies Jugal Expedition of 1955 (including Monica Jackson and Betty Stark) had crossed the Langdang, and had climbed to a beautiful clearing on a plateau above the river. To reach it they had to climb a 400-ft cliff using sections of tree-trunk ladder. This meadow, called Chintang, is the site of an ancient *gompa* that still has a resident Lama.

After crossing four major spurs and two more camps, we found a trail that appeared substantial enough to be more than an animal track, and seemed to lead to the valley. The option of staying high and trying to reach Panch Pokhari in these difficult conditions held no appeal. Instead, with food supplies now critically low, and the porters having endured more than should be expected, we descended, knowing that a trail existed (could we find it) which would lead to Tempathang.

The descent, although obviously used by people, was better suited to gibbons. Literally hanging from the branches, we swung, slipped and tumbled towards the valley through a magnificent forest of pine and larch, that lower down became large maple and magnolia interspersed with rhododendrons and thickets of bamboo which had obviously been cut for cane.

In all, the never-ending descent must have been close to 6,000 feet; it certainly felt like it. By the time we reached the valley floor, jarred and wobbly-kneed, all that kept us going was the thought that at Tempathang, a settlement peopled by Sherpa from Solu, we would find the contents for our empty pots. Finally, in near darkness, we wandered into Tempathang, and enjoyed an honest Sherpa welcome celebrated in *chang*. Close to the end of our trek, fed and physically tired, we entered our tents and the land of Catatonica!

Over the remaining days we hiked high above the Balephi on its east bank through Gompathang and Bolde, settled by Lamas (a name not only used for Buddhist monks, but also for a Sherpa clan and for Tamangs in East Nepal).

Below Gompathang, the valley of the Balephi broadens, and is heavily terraced and cultivated. Staying high above the valley the path eventually descends to the Newar settlement and suspension bridge and Phalanksangu.

After the wild and rugged country that had gone before, it came as a real surprise to wander past the well-constructed houses along the paved streets of Jalbire, with its multitude of open shops and traders. Once an important town on the trade route to Tibet, between Kathmandu and Kodari, it has now been passed by the Chinese Road and its importance has diminished.

We reached the road and the growing bazaar of Balephi the following day, from where a regular bus service leaves for Kathmandu. Seemingly a million miles distant, it was in reality only four diesel-filled hours away.

ITINERARY:

DAYS 1 – 2: KATHMANDU TO PATI BHANJYANG

Bus to Sundarijal. Ascend steeply to Shivapuri Danda through several settlements to Burlang Bhanjyang (2,438m/8,000ft). Fine views to the north. Continue on good trail to Pati Bhanjyang. Checkpost.

DAYS 3 – 4: PATI BHANJYANG TO TARKE GHYANG

Descend Talamarang Valley to Melamchi Khola — climb northwards through numerous villages on west bank. Cross river and ascend to Thimbu. Climb steeply to Tarke Ghyang.

DAYS 5 – 7: TARKE GHYANG TO SOUTH SIDE OF GANJA LA

Ascend to Dupku Danda, follow this northwards high above Yangri Khola in and out of several hollows and kharkas — Dupku, Keldang — and finally climb steeply the moraine-filled valley towards the Ganja La. Several campsites on south side. This is difficult under snow.

This provides a good base for climbs on the south side of Naya Kanga, a listed 'trekking peak'.

DAYS 8 – 9: GANJA LA TO KYANGJIN GOMPA

Cross the Ganja La and descend steeply on the north side. Naya Kanga is normally climbed from a high camp below the pass on this side. Continue down through kharka to valley floor, cross the river to reach Kyangjin.

This is a good base from which to explore the valley and to climb the small peaks on the north side.

DAY 10: KYANGJIN TO LANGSISA KHARKA

Follow Langtang Valley eastwards past airstrip through pastures and moraines to huts at Langsisa.

DAY 11 – 12: TILMAN'S PASS

Climb moraines under the east flank of Gangchempo towards Tilman's Pass (west). Campsites amongst the moraines. Cross the pass early, keeping close under the west flank of Urkinmang. Stay close to Urkinmang and descend on the south side to a remote boulder-filled valley.

DAYS 13 – 15: TILMAN'S TO TEMPATHANG

Continue south through Jugal, keeping high on the east flank of the Panch Pokhari Lekh above the Balephi Khola. Cross several spurs. Descend through dense woodland to cross the river and reach Tempathang. This is a difficult and dangerous crossing in poor conditions.

It is also possible to stay high and continue to Panch Pokhari and continue down the ridge to Chautarra or descend westwards into Helambu.

DAYS 16 – 18: TEMPATHANG TO KATHMANDU

Continue south down the Balephi Valley through many villages and towns, including Gompathang and Jalbire, along the east bank

Hiking south near Tin Pokhari along the Panche Pokhari Danda high above the Balephi Khola, with the peaks of Dorje Lhakpa (6,990m/22,993ft) beyond.

above extensive terracing. Continue south to the Chinese Road at Balephi Bazar. Bus to Kathmandu.

DIFFICULTY:

This is a strenuous and remote trek that crosses two difficult passes, one of which is quite technical and on ice. Fresh snow or poor weather would make this a potentially dangerous undertaking, especially in the upper Yamdi and Balephi Kholas.

LOGISTICS:

This is only suitable for well-equipped and supplied parties able to carry the required food and kit to remain self-supporting for the duration of the trek. Some re-supply would be possible in Langtang, although for a larger party it might be better to send food in by road to Dhunche and then on to Langtang, rather than carry everything over the Ganja La.

EQUIPMENT:

Ropes, axes and crampons are required for Tilman's. Porters will need clothing, including boots for the crossing.

MAP:

Schneider Helambu/Langtang 1:100,000. Contains many inaccuracies.

SEASON:

Post-monsoon is best, because of the old problem of late spring snow making it impossible to reach and cross the passes.

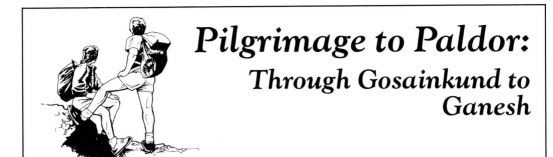

Pilgrimage to Paldor:
Through Gosainkund to Ganesh

This business of discovering passes and minor peaks is a most fascinating form of Himalayan mountaineering. The climber who cares only for capturing a big peak necessarily knows exactly where he will get to if he is successful, for the top is a blatantly obvious goal. On the other hand, the explorer of passes is often shielded from the commonplace certainty of knowing where he is likely to come out.

C.F. Meade

For the best part of a decade I had looked longingly at the Ganesh Himal, but only from afar. In the post-monsoon season of 1985 I took the chance to lead a small climbing party to Paldor, a fine trekking peak at the eastern end of that range and, as it happens, the first peak in Nepal to be climbed by Western climbers. Thus I completed a pilgrimage, and another chapter in my book on the 'trekking peaks' of Nepal.

The Ganesh Himal is named after the elephant-headed god of good fortune, images of which are found throughout the Kathmandu Valley. Seen from the capital, the main Ganesh peaks − Ganesh I (7,405m/24,968ft), Labsang Karpo (Ganesh II) (7,150m/23,458ft), Ganesh III (7,132m/23,398ft), and Papil (Ganesh IV) (7,102m/23,300ft), stand out like crystals of glistening quartz from the rank of peaks that is the 'Great Himalayan Chain', forming the skyline north of the Kathmandu valley rim.

This striking massif is contained between the immense valleys of the Buri Gandaki in the west and the Bhote Khosi in the east, which in its lower reaches becomes the Trisuli Khola. Seen from all sides, this range, although not housing any of Nepal's 8,000-metre giants, sports some impressive pyramidal peaks of snow and ice.

It was to the eastern end of this range that Bill Tilman went in 1949, when Nepal first opened its mountains to Westerners. Although at the time both he and the Mount Everest Committee may have been disappointed that their application to approach 'Big E' from the south was turned down, in the end I'm sure that Tilman was more than content with having the opportunity to roam freely up the deep valleys and along the high ridges of both Langtang and Ganesh. He was doing what he enjoyed most: travelling light over passes, exploring uncharted areas, with *carte blanche* to 'have a go' at whatever small peak took his fancy.

For much of its course, this route follows long sinuous ridges, dropping occasionally into major valleys which have to be crossed on the journey north-west to Ganesh. Although along sections of the route it would be possible for a small party to find board and lodging in private homes, it is an itinerary better suited to the self-sufficient, staying as it does away from the well-trekked trails. It is only around Pati Bhanjyang and Syabrubensi that popular trekking routes are crossed and *bhattis* plentiful. The outstanding feature of this trek for me is the almost constant

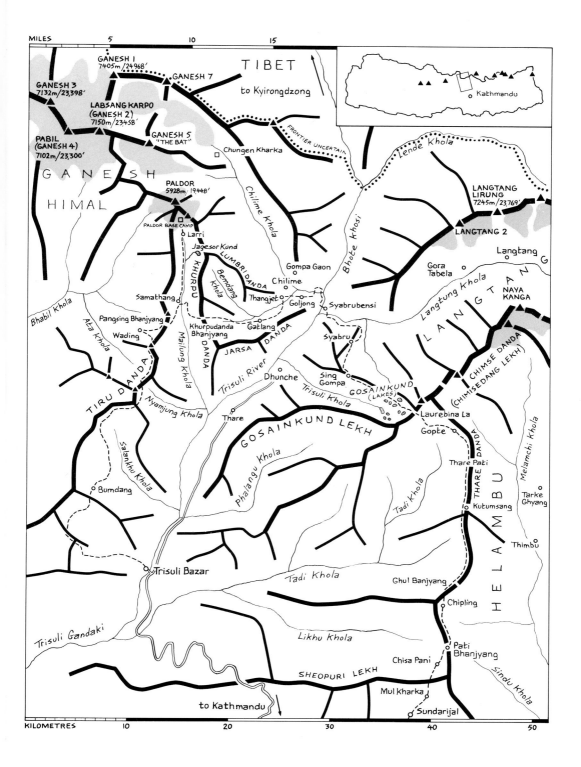

MILES

5 10 15

GANESH 1
7405m /24,968'

GANESH 7

TIBET

to Kyirongdzong

GANESH 3
7132m/23,398'

LABSANG KARPO
(GANESH 2)
7150m/23,458'

GANESH 5
"THE BAT"

Chungen Kharka

FRONTIER UNCERTAIN

Lende Khola

Kathmandu

PABIL
(GANESH 4)
7102m/23,300'

G A N E S H

HIMAL

PALDOR
5928m, 19,448'

PALDOR BASE CAMP

Larri

Jagesor Kund

Bhabil Khola

Samathang

Pangsing Bhanjyang

Wading

KHURPU

LUMBRIDANDA

Bemdang Khola

Chilime Khola

Gompa Gaon

Chilime

Thangjet

Goljong

Syabrubensi

Bhote Khosi

LANGTANG
LIRUNG
7245m/23,769'

LANGTANG 2

Langtang

Gora
Tabela

Langtang Khola

NAYA
KANGA

L A N G T A N G

Ata Khola

Mailung Khola

Khurpudanda
Bhanjyang

JARSA

Gatlang

DANDA

Syabru

Dhunche

Sing
Gompa

GOSAINKUND
(LAKES)

Laurebina La

CHIMSE DANDA
(CHIMISEDANG LEKH)

Melamchi Khola

TIRU DANDA

Nyamjung Khola

Thare

Trisuli River

Trisuli Khola

GOSAINKUND LEKH

Gopte

Thare Pati

THARE DANDA

Tarke
Ghyang

Salankhu Khola

Bumdang

Phalangu Khola

Tadi Khola

Kutumsang

H E L A M B U

Thimbu

Trisuli Bazar

Tadi Khola

Ghul Banjyang

Chipling

Trisuli Gandaki

Likhu Khola

Chisa Pani

Pati
Bhanjyang

Sindu Khola

SHEOPURI LEKH

Mul kharka

to Kathmandu

Sundarijal

KILOMETRES 10 20 30 40 50

Moonrise above the flank of Ganesh looking eastwards across the Buri Gandaki from Base Camp on Himalchuli.

views of the Greater Himalaya, extending from the Annapurnas to Choba Bhamare and the Lumding Himal beyond.

The fastest route into Paldor on the eastern side of Ganesh is up the Trisuli Valley, now, alas, spoilt for trekking by a bulldozed road that extends as far as Dhunche. My preference was to tramp the Thare Danda, an exceptional ridge walk north of Pati Bhanjyang. It borders the Sherpa settlements of Helambu, and leads in three glorious days, with endless views of Langtang and Jugal, to a rough campsite at the head of the Tadi Khola known as 'Gopte's Cave'. In fact *gopte* is a corruption of the Nepali word for cave, which here turns out to be little more than an overhanging boulder. From camp the view south towards the Shivapuri Ridge and beyond to the Mahabharat Lekh was one of endless blue hills, horizon after horizon fading into the palest hue until earth and heaven merged.

It would have been possible to have made Gosainkund in a long day from *gopte*. Instead I decided to camp below the Laurebina La (4,608m/15,120ft), to prolong living in the wilderness. From an early start it was then possible to cross the pass and descend awkward snow slopes past small frozen tarns above the main lake of Gosainkund. A fresh dusting of snow over the rocks, now in bright sunlight, made the deep azure waters of the lake sparkle as though encrusted with gems. We skirted the lake's northern shore, past a small cluster of buildings and a lingum shrine. During the full moon in the monsoon months of August, this becomes the focus of thousands of pilgrims who visit these sacred lakes to worship Shiva during the festival of Janai Purne. The belief is that Shiva, having drunk poison, thrust his trident into the mountainside, making water pour from the hill to form the lakes from which he drank to slake his thirst.

In a thousand ages of the Gods, I could not tell thee of the glories of Himalchal, where Shiva lived and where the Ganges falls from the throne of Vishnu like the slender thread of a Lotus flower.

By bathing in the lakes a follower gains merit. Alas, on this cold November morning I'm afraid I gained none!

We traversed an airy path high above the other lakes of the trilogy — Bhairavkund, and Saraswatikund with its plunging waterfall, 'like the slender thread of a Lotus flower'. The trail led to a superb open ridge that provided clear views of Ganesh Himal and beyond to another stunning trinity; the peaks of Himalchuli, Peak 29 and Manaslu. Avoiding the direct route to Syabru, we continued down the ridge crest, flanking the Trisuli Khola to visit Sing Gompa (3,524m/10,675ft) and to buy curds at the HMG cheese factory at Chenchenbari. These have sprung up all over highland Nepal and have been the direct result of a Swiss Aid Programme very much influenced by Toni Hagen's visits in the 1950s. The cheese they produce, and especially the curds and *lassi*, when they are available, are superb, and I'm always willing to hike out of my way to get some.

Sadly, the hillside before the *gompa* has been devastated by fire, and the path now meanders through a forest of blackened tree trunks standing like ghastly totems, stark against the distant snows.

Syabru (2,118m/6,950ft) is the meeting of the ways. The path from Dhunche to Langtang passes through the village, the home of Sherpas and Tamangs who farm the steep terraced hillsides above the Langtang Khola, and graze animals on the high pastures towards Laurebina. Its shingle-roofed houses and lodges, built down the spine of a narrow spur, terraced one above the other, reminded me of the overlapping scales of a huge reptile.

From Syabru we followed the track down through the village past a great tree. At a chorten, our path diverted left through terraced fields, and continued steadily down over a thinly-forested, craggy hillside, crossing the Langtang Khola by a modern suspension bridge at Syabrubensi.

After the relatively wild trekking through Gosainkund, it comes as a shock to descend towards the Bhote Khosi and see on the far hillside the devastation caused by deforestation and the building of a new road. This will eventually connect (if it hasn't already) Trisuli Bazar with the upper Mailung Khola. The result is a shocking scar of newly-exposed rock and eroding soil.

Rounding the end of the hillside, we contoured north up the Bhote Khosi valley which, further south, below its confluence with the Langtang Khola, becomes the Trisuli Gandaki. Traditionally this valley was a trade route into Tibet, connecting Kathmandu via Trisuli with Kyirongdzong, where Heinrich Harrer and Peter Aufschnaiter in 1944 went several months after their escape from Dehra Dun. A short way upstream on another swaying suspension bridge, with holes where there should have been planking, we crossed to the west bank glimpsing the rumbling river far below. A short distance downstream there are some derelict mine buildings, and below these a sulphurous hot spring gurgles from the hillside, affording the opportunity for a smelly bath. Incidentally, it is possible to find a line of these springs running diagonally across Nepal, each slightly further upstream as you journey west from this valley. I have tested those in the Buri Gandaki, Marsyangdi Khola and the Kali Gandaki, and only the Buri baths rated a 10; but then it did come after a particularly leech-ridden day! I assume this geo-thermal activity occurs along a fault line.

We turned north over the bridge hoping to find a path climbing the Jarsa Danda to Gholjong, certainly marked on the Mandala trekking maps. Instead, we gained the valley of the Chilime Khola and headed west to the large village of Thangjet, not marked on the recent Schneider map of Langtang and Helambu. (In fact, this whole section of the Schneider map turns out to be fairly inaccurate with regard to the siting of bridges, path position and small villages.)

In the autumn we trekked through terraced fields heavy with crops being harvested by ruddy-cheeked girls. Wielding small sickles they would appear and disappear like the Cheshire cat's smile in various parts of the field; bobbing to cut the waist-high millet, against a backcloth of *chortens* that mark the trail north towards Chilime and Gompa Gaon.

At Thangjet the Chilime Khola meandered north between the Lumbri Danda and the Thungmau Kulen Bangarchehan. This was the route explored by Tilman in 1949 and is the obvious approach to the east side of Ganesh, particularly The Bat or Ganesh V (6,950m/ 22,802ft).

Our route continued roughly westwards, following the course of the Bemdang Khola through Sungbati to Gatlang, where the trail climbs through intricately-terraced hillsides along a path held between dry-stone walls. At the time, with head dropped watching my feet in concentration and effort, it was easy to imagine I was back home in the Yorkshire Dales, plodding the green road of Mastiles Lane. But if you stop for a moment, rest your pack on a *chautarra* or *mani* wall and look back, you make a quantum leap, far from the striding Dales. There, at the end of the valley, rising above the shadowy depths of the Bhote Khosi, is the awesome bulk of Langtang Lirung (7,245m/ 23,769ft), first climbed by a joint Japanese/ Nepali expedition in 1978.

All along this trail, throughout a brilliant blue sky day, the mantra of the *mani* stones carved in glistening mica-schist, echoed the glare of the summit snows, and lines from *As You Like It*.

And this our life exempt from public haunt
Finds tongues in trees, books in the running brooks,
Sermons in stones and good in everything.
I would not change it.

As we neared Gatlang, thunderous explosions from the road builders on the Jarsa Danda had us scrambling for shelter, as blocks and boulders bounded down the hillside, crashing through trees and scrub.

Gatlang is obviously a prosperous community; they have well-planned terraced fields with abundant crops and large herds of animals. Goats, cows and bovine-crosses are tended by round-faced, well-fed children in what looked to be a mixture of typical Tamang and Tibetan dress with very little evidence of Western influence. Their cloth, mostly coarse woollen fustian made on a narrow backstrap loom and dyed purple, is stitched together to make broader cloth not by a thin thread but by rough twine. On their heads they wear not the typical Nepali *topi*, but a squat, circular cap with an upturned, decorated brim. The Gatlangba are not a friendly bunch, and their black dogs, roaming freely, barked and growled a welcome. Even the trail was directed up and around the village rather than through it, so that the stone and timber houses huddling closely together seemed to smoulder as the fire-smoke seeped through their blackened shingles into the clear air.

Beyond the stone and timber houses the trail continued to climb through terraces until at last the path reached the tree-line. In 1985 the army had established a semi-permanent camp in the forest, from where they directed road-building ordnance and communications. Again, our permits were checked and, despite our very non-military appearance, we were given a most hospitable welcome and stayed for some time chatting to the officer, encircled by the grinning faces of the other ranks. It's always a little disconcerting trying to reconcile the image of the *kukri*-wielding warrior with the gentle vision of the hand-holding squaddies one sees throughout Nepal.

Beyond the encampment the forest deepened and the trail led us steeply towards an unseen pass on the Khurpu Danda. There are small clearings in the forest but level campsites are few and far between, although about an hour above the army camp we did find a reasonable clearing, Yuri Kharka, with a plentiful supply of water and dead wood. After the enclosed forest, reaching the Khurpu Danda Bhanjyang was a delightful contrast. This high ridge running north to Ganesh Himal separates the waters of the Bemdang from the Mailung Khola, giving exceptional views of the Langtang Himal and to the mountains beyond Langtang in Tibet; in particular you can see the peaks of Kyungka Ri and Shishapangma (the highest mountain wholly in Chinese-occupied Tibet, and the last 8,000-metre peak to be climbed).

Looking to the west, across the heavily-forested Mailung Khola, we could see the serpentine ridge of the Tiru Danda. Directly opposite, although slightly higher, was the Pansing Bhanjyang (3,856m/12,651ft) and the route of the return leg of our Paldor Expedition.

Despite the new road being built into the Mailung Khola, this valley rarely sees trekkers, for although the trail passes through numerous small villages there are no tourist lodges as such after Syabrubensi. Between Gatlang and the villages south of the Tiru Danda there is no possibility of re-supply or inhabited settlements until the Salankhu Khola, although an alternative route is possible via the Ankhu Valley further west.

For a short while at least after the pass on the Khurpu Danda the trail stays high, following the ridge northwards, skirting the precipitous crest on its west flank. In places the trail is exciting, passing steeply through several rocky notches before descending gradually to the valley floor. Inevitably it meets the new track which can be

Images of Ganesh, the elephant-headed god, can be seen all over the Kathmandu Valley.

followed through a fine fir forest to another small army post and checkpoint at Samathang. This is not marked on the Schneider map but is located slightly north of where the track connecting the Khurpu Danda Bhanjyang with the Pansing Bhanjyang crosses the Mailung Khola.

Ahead was our goal. At the end of the valley there is a marked step above which, in what might be termed a hanging valley, is the Paldor cwm — a small mountain amphitheatre. The cwm is dominated by the south-west face of Paldor, and a host of satellite peaks and glaciers, along with the Jagesor Kund, a small lake trapped in the moraines below the mountain.

We trekked northwards up the true right bank of the river on a narrow jewel of a path. The path is quite literally 'jewelled', because it is studded with faceted garnets that can be picked from the metamorphic schistose rock.

A Sherpani above the deep blue water of sacred Gosainkund — 'where the Ganges falls from the throne of Vishnu like the slender thread of a Lotus flower'.

Now on the true left bank of the river, the path climbs steeply towards the small mine at Larri. We spent some time chatting to the manager about what was being dug, but to no avail. There wasn't a lot of activity from underground but it is obviously important enough for the construction of the road and we wondered whether we would thereafter 'glow in the dark'! In fact, it turns out to be nothing more exciting than manganese. It's a worrying thought that in the future the road might result in extensive logging and subsequent deforestation of the beautiful Mailung Valley.

Beyond the mine, the path is unrelenting and we scrambled above the narrow Mailung Gorge around a fine rocky pinnacle (Ned's Thumb).

Our small party were intent on climbing Paldor and hoped to find the odd new route on other summits. Amongst the party was Ronnie Faux who, apart from being an enthusiastic sailor and single malt drinker, is reasonably good on snow and ice. As Messner's biographer and co-author of *Soldiers on Everest,* he had a wealth of outrageous stories. The oldest member of the party, George Fowler, was also one of the fittest. Having achieved three-score years he was well on his way to gathering the other ten. George had been with me on an arduous trip through the Hongu and Hinku and had an unquenchable longing for the hills. (His son, Mick Fowler, takes after the 'old man' in his taste for adventure and is at the forefront of British mountaineering.) As it happened, both these members of the team (unbeknown to each other) worked for *The Times* newspaper. Ronnie, a reporter for over twenty years, was the Scottish Correspondent, with a brief to cover 'adventure', whilst George worked in the print shop (when the paper had one), keeping the presses running. In the end both made it to the summit of Paldor, despite the difficult conditions, negotiated without strike or disputes of any kind . . .

We established our Base Camp in deep snow, below a rocky peak christened 'Ned's Thumb' in 1975 by John Cleare — a fine mountain with an inappropriate name. It was obvious because of the amount of snow that many of our plans for romping around the small summits encircling the Paldor glaciers would have to be shelved, and our efforts should be concentrated on the peak itself. The day after our arrival, George and I went off to explore The Thumb and the high col behind base to get a feel for conditions. Happy with the snow quality and our own acclimatization, we returned to camp from the summit late in the day.

Over the next two days we established a High Camp on the Paldor Glacier East, in a beautiful basin fringed with delightful rocky aiguilles.

Following the course of an ablation stream beside a lateral moraine we found a good site for Base Camp. For a climbing party this is a splendid base as the area bristles with numerous summits that can be climbed in Alpine style. For the adventurous trekker who has a taste for scrambling there's plenty to explore and discover in this wild amphitheatre.

Camp looked southwards towards the Mailung Khola, filled, as the sun set, by crimson-tinged clouds lapping against the valleys walls; it was a perfect pitch.

At a desperate hour when the body's system is at its lowest, the alarm shocked me into consciousness. I shouted to the other tents and fumbled about dressing inside my sleeping bag, reluctant to go out into the cold. Ready eventually, we forced down warm drinks and biscuits, shivering beneath a sky unbelievably full of stars. From camp we traversed the glacier northwards towards a headwall that formed the containing rim of the glacier basin. A low point on the rim is the divide between our glacier and a stream system draining into the Chilime Khola. Rising over a series of rocky outcrops from this col is the narrow ice crest of Paldor's

East Ridge, first climbed by Tilman, Lloyd and Tensing in June 1949. The snow was frozen hard and our crampons screeched as we tramped towards the flank of the ridge. Avalanche runnels had cut the lip of the bergschrund, bridging its gaping mouth with solid snow. We climbed diagonally over sun-cupped and dimpled ice towards a rock pinnacle left of the col. Below the ridge strange sastrugi etched the surface like fishfins, providing holds and steps up which we climbed to the narrow crest.

Just before sunrise a cold wind howled over the ridge, forcing us into our hoods and silence. From a final rocky step the ridge led horizontally at first, before rising steeply in an ultimate leap to the summit, but the summit wasn't given — it had to be won. With a sting in its tail, the firm ridge gave way to a wall of ice covered by knee-

The houses of Syabru cling to the ridge like the scales of a great beast.

deep powder. Each step had to be sculpted from the sugary snow — heavy-booted yob tactics had no place here, only precise footwork yielded an upward step. At last, after three hard-won rope lengths, a final wind-blown cornice, like old meringue, gave way to the horizontal summit. We tap-danced on the top, looking at the incredible panorama eastwards, where Shishapangma's bulk was unmistakable beyond the Langtang Himal. Finally, cold forced an inevitable retreat to High Camp and Base.

Our return trek from Jagesor Kung and Paldor Base Camp retraced the walk-in as far as Samathang before climbing through forest towards the Pansing Bhanjyang. This was a good trail, obviously used by herders from Tipling as a kind of drove road to other pastures. Once we were out of the forest, the vista opened up with the Langtang peaks and the Chimisedang Lekh appearing over the Khurpu Danda. Having reached a high point near 3,000 metres the path contours after a fashion — an airy fashion — over precipitous drops and deep-cut re-entrants. The hillside, no longer wooded, supports coarse grasses, dwarf rhododendrons and an abundance of alpine flowers. This is raptor country, and as we hiked griffon vultures quartered the hillside, effortlessly rising and falling with the thermals, their flight echoing the contours. Just before the pass a pasture and comfortable *goth* (herder's hut) provided a delightful camp and comfortable quartering for porters.

If you have a day to spare, time should be set aside to traverse the Marsyung Danda to the north to where it divides into the ridges of the Yam Dharva and the Paldor. I think this is one of the most delightful ridge walks anywhere, with views of an array of peaks from the Annapurnas in the west, followed by Himalchuli, Peak 29 and Manaslu, through the Ganesh Himal due north, to the Langtang and Tibetan mountains further east. Depending on the season, you can expect to find some snow on this and most of the other high ridges mentioned. The early spring is the time when there's a lot of snow about, perhaps making the ridges impossible for trekking, whereas in November only a few residual snow-patches in shady hollows are likely.

For lovers of high and wild places the next two days were a delight. From the col we followed, as near as possible, the crest of the Tiru Danda which, for a while at least, has springy downland turf on its western flank. Although it would be possible to traverse the ridge in a day to a kharka at the southern end, I opted to descend from the ridge to a herder's *goth* at Wading. We reached it by a mossy trail, descending westwards through dense forest to a clearing with fresh water, wood and shelter. Best of all, it offered stunning views across the Bhabil Khola to the southern flank of Ganesh.

Across the tree tops, from the clearing, the not-so-distant Lapsang Karpo, along with Ganesh I and V, thrust through a sea of cloud. As we sat by the fire with our Sherpas and porters, a full mottled moon rose, lighting both the cloud and the eternal snows. It was an unforgettable evening with only the intense cold finally driving me to my tent.

It was also the time of an incident which highlights the sense of duty of the best Sirdars and Sherpas. So impressive was the night with the sky full of stars and the mountains lit by a full moon, that I decided a time-exposure was needed to capture the scene and trace the apparent arc of the stars across the sky. Not far from my tent I set up my tripod and camera, tripped the shutter, leaving it open, and went to sleep, with an alarm set to wake me when the exposure I had calculated had got the image. Half an hour or so later I was aware of something rustling at the door of my tent, and got up to investigate. It was Ang Dali Sherpa doing a last round of the camp, making sure that everything was safe, tucking my camera and tripod inside

the tent! Amused and just a little annoyed I rushed around, all but naked, setting the shot again. Resetting the alarm, I went shivering back to my pit. Several hours later, digital bleeps intruded into a deep sleep. I pulled on a sweater and emerged reluctantly from my cocoon only to find, tucked inside the tent flysheet, my camera, all safe and sound, recording for posterity the utter darkness of the tent interior. It was a long night, never to be recorded on film. The Sherpa had been sent to make sure all was safe about camp; he had done his duty.

From Wading we regained the Tiru Danda at a small pass in perfect post-monsoon weather. Crystal-clear mountains sat in a deep blue sky with fluffy cumulus floating aimlessly above the greener hills.

The ridge path is followed, in places quite steeply, along the crest, rising and falling to gain small pinnacles and sharp notches. In springtime this trek must be ablaze with colour as the flanks of the ridge are an impenetrable jungle of rhododendrons.

At its southern end the Tiru Danda bends westwards, separating the headwaters of the Ata Khola and the Nyamjung Khola, until at last at a clearing the ridge-top track ends. This final high viewpoint is spectacular with precipitous drops into dark forests, and beyond to the north-west the unmistakable mass of Himalchuli, Manaslu and Peak 29.

At first the route appeared to have reached an *impasse;* the ridge ahead curving away to the west was split by a profound notch (marked on some maps as the Singla Bhanjyang), into which the path now descended steeply between several vegetated pinnacles. From the notch the trail continued southwards to a clearing at Rupchet, where we made a comfortable camp overlooking the deep valley of the Nyamjung.

The following morning the trail continued to contour and fall to the valley of the Salankhu Khola in deep forest teeming with birdlife. Not only birds! As I walked through the forest, chatting with a Sherpa, we were alarmed by what we thought was a boulder avalanching through the dense undergrowth above. We were surprised when, a metre or so in front of us, a Himalayan bear rolled on to the path, stood up, as wide-eyed as ourselves, and then tumbled off again into the steep undergrowth below.

For the next couple of days we trekked slowly through terraced farmland in the Salankhu basin. Ways east towards the Trisuli valley and Betrawati offered themselves, but were rejected in favour of the rarely-trekked paths, leading eventually through Bumdang to the valley of the Samrie Khola and the traditional east-west trade route between Ghurka and Trisuli Bazar. The trail into Trisuli shocks as vehicles, electric lights and the fashions of the West, in the colours of the East, inflict another reality.

ITINERARY:

This takes no account of rest days, climbing or exploration.

(Left) Tamang girls in the Chilime Khola near Gatlang with the bulk of Langtang Lirung (7,245m/23,769ft) rising above the shadowy depths of the Bhote Khosi.

DAY 1: KATHMANDU TO PATI BHANJYANG
Vehicle to Sundarijal — climb out of valley to Shivapuri Ridge and Burlang Bhanjyang (2,438m/8,000ft). Good camping and splendid views.

DAYS 2 – 3: PATI BHANJYANG TO GOPTE
Fine open walking along Thare Danda.

Glorious and extensive views. Small villages and kharkas. Traverse head of Tadi Khola to camp at Gopte Cave.

DAYS 4 – 5: GOPTE TO SYABRU

Cross Laurebina La East, descend to Gosainkund, continue to Sing Gompa in a long day. Descend to Syabru. I prefer to take three days' camping below Laurebina La on Tadi Khola side, to enjoy the fantastic country.

DAYS 6 – 9: SYABRU TO MAILUNG KHOLA

Descend Langtang Khola to Syabrubensi. Cross Bhote Khosi (hot springs), go north, turn into Chilime Khola to Thangjet (STOL airstrip). Continue westwards through Tamang villages to Gatlang. Climb to Khurpu Danda Bhanjyang camp at Yuri Kharka. Cross into Mailung Khola camp below Larri mine.

DAY 10: PALDOR BASE CAMP

Climb steeply past mine into wild glacier cwm. Camp in moraines.

This provides an ideal base from which to explore or climb.

DAY 11: BASE CAMP TO PANSING BHANJYANG

Descend to Somdang in Mailung Khola and ascend to kharka below Pansing Bhanjyang.

DAY 12: EXPLORE TIRU DANDA NORTH OF PANSING BHANJYANG

Glorious ridge-walking and views.

DAYS 13 – 14: TIRU DANDA TO RUPCHET KHARKA

Follow Tiru Danda south. Descend to Rupchet kharka. Spectacular walking and views.

DAYS 15 – 17: RUPCHET TO TRISULI

Good trekking through cultivated terraced farmland, including the settlements of Gonga, Bhalche and Bumdang to Samri Khola and Trisuli Bazar.

ALTERNATIVE ROUTE FROM PANSING BHANJYANG

Should the snows on the Tiru Danda prove too much, or poor weather force a retreat to lower ground, there is an alternative, or a contrasting return trek from the Pansing Bhanjyang, that is highly recommended.

From the campsites at the Pansing Bhanjyang kharka, gain the pass, marked by a *chorten* and *mani* stones, from where the views are extensive and spectacular. Drop down the west side by a steep narrow path littered with snowdrops in the spring, and enter attractive forests to a kharka (9,900ft). The trail thereafter continues less steep but at times quite rocky to the edge of the trees after a wonderful forest walk. Below, the trail descends through dusty terraces first to Lapdung and then to Tipling Gaon (2,000m/ 6,561ft), before descending very steeply into the Bhabil Khola gorge (Linju Khola on some maps), at the bottom of which there are some fine bathing pools. After this a dusty climb of almost 300 metres leads to Serthung (1,981m/6,500ft).

The aim is to gain the main Ankhu Valley, which is reached by a quite spectacular path, which descends steeply in places through terraced hillsides joining a trail from Singla Bhanjyang shortly before the village of Barung (1,372m/5,400ft). Below is the confluence of the Ankhu and Bhabil (Manjar) Kholas. The trail now continues southwards in the main valley, staying high on the true left bank. For much of the time the way is through terraces, occasional woods and small villages, including Jhorlang. In places the trail is quite difficult, with areas of rough, loose ground and at least two major landslides to cross, after which campsites are few and far between.

Shortly afterwards you enter the gorge of the Churing Khola, bedecked with steep crags and vertiginous forest. The stream provides an ideal spot to wash away the dust of terrace bashing!

After a cool, refreshing swim, there is a hot and sweaty climb out of the gorge and again through terraces to the village of Khuri

Hill children with vast baskets out collecting animal fodder.

(1,645m/5,400ft), which, incidentally, is wrongly marked on the Mandala maps. The way ahead continues through terraced hill country as far as Dharka (1,706m/5,600ft), following the contour of the main Ankhu Valley. After the village the route curls round the spur into the valley of the Chimtang Khola, passing numerous small hamlets not marked on the map, before descending into the river's gorge. After crossing the river and making the steep climb out of the gorge, numerous possibilities for a good overnight camp can be found.

Ahead, the route continues to climb steeply again through terraced farmland to the strung-out village of Chimtang (1,706m/5,600ft). Beyond, the trail crosses scrubby hillside and enters an attractive forested valley dappled with open glades. The path leads to a bridge after which the trail again climbs steeply through forest to Mergang Bhanjyang (2,081m/6,830ft), where the superb south flank of an airy ridge dotted with rhododendrons leads eventually to the village of Dhurale (1,640m/5,380ft). Below, the trail from Bumdang and the Tiru Danda is joined and followed to Trisuli Bazar.

DIFFICULTY:

This is a long and strenuous trek although without technical difficulty. Much of it is along fine ridges. Snow might persist on some of the high passes and narrow ridges, especially in early spring or soon after the monsoon. Paldor

Ronnie Faux walking amongst the clouds on his way to High Camp on Paldor.

is an official trekking peak requiring a permit and mountaineering skills.

LOGISTICS:

Public buses to Bodanath. Private buses to Sundarijal. Porters should be engaged in Kathmandu. Vehicles go to Dhunche in the Trisuli valley, one day's trek from Syabrubensi. Daily buses between Trisuli and Kathmandu (4 hours). To complete the trek as described, parties need to be self-sufficent. There are few lodges *en route*.

EQUIPMENT:

No specialist equipment is required for the trek. Those wishing to climb Paldor will obviously need specialist technical climbing equipment. (*See Trekking Peaks of Nepal*, Bill O'Connor, Crowood Press 1989.)

SEASON AND WEATHER:

Late April to early May is a stunning time for the trek, as the alpine flowers and the rhododendrons are in full bloom, although afternoon clouds sometimes tend to obscure the more distant views. Early spring might present problems of too much snow on the high ridges. Post-monsoon on the other hand would give settled weather and absolute clarity, although in November and December the nights can be cold.

MAPS:

Covered by the Mandala Trekking Map Helambu, Gosainkund, Langtang 1:125,000 sheet. The first part of the trek is also covered on the 1987 Schneider Helambu/Langtang 1:100,00 sheet, although I've found this quite misleading and inaccurate.

Through Hell and High Water:
Up the Buri Gandaki to Himalchuli

As I stepped out on my first day's march in the Himalayas, a strange exhilaration thrilled me. I kept squeezing my fists together and saying emphatically to myself and to the universe at large: 'Oh yes! Oh yes! This is really splendid! How splendid! How splendid!

Francis Younghusband

Bangladesh Biman's international flight made a pogo-stick landing at Dacca, screeching along the concrete before turning sharply to taxi towards the terminal. I could see a million faces on the viewing gantry passively eyeing the plane. It required a 'clean and jerk' to raise my carry-on holdall to my shoulder. Risking a hernia, I staggered as nonchalantly as possible towards the exit. A baggage allowance of 20 kilos isn't enough to sustain a jet trekker in the 'global village', let alone a mountaineer *en route* to join his expedition.

It hit me squarely between the eyes as I left the plane; like a blow from a heavyweight boxer, the oppressive heat and total humidity sweeping in from the Bay of Bengal left me gasping and sweat-soaked within seconds. I felt ridiculous, dressed in double boots, sweaters and duvet, surrounded by half-naked porters vying for the odd rupee that might ensure they would reach the bread-line.

'Excuse me. Where do I check in for the Kathmandu flight?'

I was standing in front of a harassed man wearing a uniform (of sorts), who was marshalling a wad of papers — he appeared to represent order in a scene depicting chaos. He was quite possibly deaf.

'Excuse me, where do I check in for Kathmandu?' This time louder and more clearly.

'Vhot is it you are saying?' replied the harassed man.

Armed with an official piece of paper prepared by my travel agent, I pointed at my onward connection to Kathmandu and repeated my question. Now he looked even more tormented, his face taking on a pained expression as if to share the grief he knew his answer would cause, his head wobbling from side to side.

'Scuse me, but I am very sorry indeed sar, that is not possible.'

'What do you mean, not possible? I've got a flight to catch, an expedition to join, and,' even more grandly, 'a mountain to climb.'

The little man looked even more distressed. His face creased like a concertina under the anguish. He fingered his papers, now wrinkled and dirty with nervous handling, as if they were the official worry beads of a paper-pushing wallah. I could feel that he wanted to say something I wanted to hear, and indeed I wanted him to say something I wanted to hear. Alas, with the best will in the world he couldn't bring himself to say it.

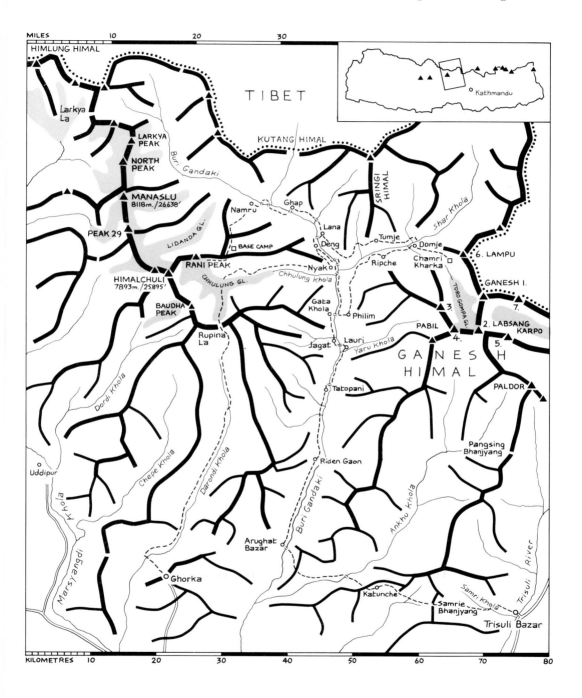

'Kathmandu flight going yesterday — next time going in four days. I am very sorry sar.'

So was I. Despite the fact that they had listed a connecting flight to Kathmandu, it was a fiction, put there merely to fill out the page — an exercise in time-tabling. There was no way at the time, with the aircraft it had, that Biman could have flown its published schedule. But all this knowledge is with hindsight and at the time I was motivated more by a cheap ticket than a certificate of airworthiness, or indeed aircraft. My four days in Bangladesh had an effect; I was considerably lighter, and I left with memories of bicycles and fine faces full of hopelessness deeply etched in my mind.

By the time I reached Kathmandu the other members of the British Himalchuli Expedition had departed for the mountain. There was a note waiting for me from Ian Howell and John Cleare, the joint leaders.

Dear Bill,

Sorry to hear about your delay, assumed you arrived safely. We have left you with the job of clearing the radios, there was a slight hold-up at the ministry which we are sure you can sort out.

Our small army of porters will be moving slowly, so you should catch us up quickly in the Buri. Have fun!

Bergheil . . .

John and Pin

This missive left me depressed. I'd had enough of paper-shufflers and offices, and longed to be on expedition. In the morning I went along to the Ministry to sort out my trekking permit. It was closed. I called at another office to sort out the remaining load still being held at customs; it was also closed. In fact, all offices were closed — it was an official holiday! Kathmandu has many of them and the traveller should beware. If all the gods and demi-gods of the Hindu and Buddhist pantheon were honoured with a holiday (and sometimes I think they are), Nepal would be a permanent carnival.

When the offices re-opened I was more relaxed, and even a little philosophical about it all. I arrived early at the Ministry, wanting to be at the head of the queue. My papers, I felt, were in order and all that was required was a rubber stamp, or perhaps a signature flashed on the page like a scimitar, to cut through the red tape binding our walkie-talkies in the Customs shed.

I sat in a hallway alongside an obese Indian businessman moaning bitterly about the inefficiency of things in Nepal, and complaining that it was almost impossible to conduct honest business since he didn't know who to bribe! Eventually my *chitti* was stamped, which allowed me to move through the curtain into another corridor and wait. Finally, I was ushered through another curtain into a small cool office. Behind a wall of papers, ink pads and rubber stamps, a diminutive, fine-featured man in a white shirt, black waistcoat and traditional *topi* sat at his desk, smiling. I explained the situation with the radios and handed over my own wad of papers.

'You have not a problem here,' he said reassuringly. I smiled back and gave a sigh of relief, feeling confident that my more philosophical, passive approach to red tape would untie the Gordian knot.

'But first you get it signed here on page number two,' he said, turning the page, and pointing with a sweeping rather than jabbing gesture of his delicate hands.

I managed to hold my smile and ask politely where I had to go for the signature. He gave me the name of a ministry and explained that it was near the National Stadium! I left, with my smile, taking a taxi to the Ministry and joined another queue, armed with a new *chitti* and my wad of papers. The rubber stamp ritual was repeated and I eventually found my way to a desk fortified with files and an ancient type-

*Seen from the Tiru Danda on the walk-out from Paldor, the peaks of Gurkha Himal —
(left to right) Baudha (6,672m/21,890ft), Himalchuli (7,893m/25,896ft), Peak 29
(7,835m/25,705ft) and Manaslu (8,156m/26,760ft) — soar above the Buri Gandaki.*

writer. After a polite conversation about my country and his country, I was duly stamped and rushed from the building back to the first ministry. It was closed and would remain so for the rest of the day, no doubt to give them time to sort their papers and ink their stamps.

In the morning I was first in and well versed in procedure. New *chitti* in hand I collected my set of stamps and gained access to the inner sanctum. Mr Narayan greeted me traditionally and formally. Triumphantly, I handed him my papers. Meanwhile, the King and Queen peered down at us from the wall through heavy-framed spectacles, as if to witness the procedure. In due course Mr Narayan signed his name on the dotted line and picked up the official final rubber stamp. I smiled triumphantly as he pressed the stamp with his gentle hand — but went cold when it left no mark.

Wobbling his head, it was now his turn to force a smile as he spat on the ink pad with all the dignity that spitting allows. Forcing the stamp into the ink he smashed it on to the form, grinding its impression into the paper, wobbling his head and muttering, 'Dam bloody ink pad no good.'

When it comes to cutting through red tape, there are times when the sword is mightier than the rubber stamp.

By the time I got to the Customs shed, force not philosophy was uppermost in my mind. Like Mr Narayan I needed to make my mark, and had quickly learned that if you want to wait patiently, they let you. I assumed that with the forms duly signed and stamped I simply needed to claim my baggage. The man behind the desk at the Customs was smiling — an ominous sign. I gave him the form, he stamped it and gave it to a dubious character who disappeared with it into the shed. I waited patiently for a very long time, the man behind the desk still smiling. Other forms were stamped and other characters entered the shed. Some actually reappeared, carrying bundles of bedding, baskets of chickens and transistor radios the size of suitcases. My man did not emerge. I went over to the smiling rubber stamp wallah, and offered to help look for our walkie-talkies.

Inside was an inferno. The long, low, dimly-lit building was unventilated and stacked from floor to ceiling with baggage, bundles and containers. There had been no attempt at order, with particular piles relating to specific flights that in turn would correspond to a wad of paper duly signed and stamped. Instead, the little men roamed about the building, lifting this parcel, climbing over that crate, removing a box from here and throwing it there in the hope that something would turn up! Eventually our box did and I left, dirty and frustrated, but not before the smiling man had rubber-stamped my papers.

Buying fruit from a woman on the trail from Trisuli.

In the early hours of the morning I left Kathmandu aboard a public bus bound for Trisuli Bazaar in the company of Ang Kami, a Sherpa from Solu. Despite the hordes, I managed to cram on to a seat which I shared with an extended family and a circus of fleas! We coughed, jolted and scratched our way westwards so that by the time we crossed the Trisuli Khola I was playing host to far more than the family's infants were.

Carrying my fair share of the load, I set off with Ang Kami from Trisuli following the trade route westwards that connects with Ghorka. A wise man would have hired another porter and travelled more swiftly. Instead, I sweated and laboured in the wake of my young Sherpa who ploughed a sharp furrow along the monsoon-muddy path. Walking in at the end of the rains is always a bit of a gamble. Given that it allows you the maximum amount of time on your mountain, it can also be hell if the weather is poor and right now it was. It rained every day,

and when it wasn't raining it looked as though it was about to. The rain is bearable, just, but the paths become treacherous; a helter-skelter of death-defying descents and hairy traverses, whilst every rest stop provides the entertaining ritual of 'hunt the leech'. It seemed that every branch and blade of grass provided the springboard for a jack-knifing bloodsucker, resulting in a lunchtime record of fourteen attached to various parts of my anatomy. By the time we reached Arughat bazaar and turned north into the valley of the Buri Gandaki, my feet were blistered, my stomach problems had returned, and I would shortly be needing a transfusion because of blood loss to leeches!

'Ang Kami. Ask at the next village when the expedition went through — there's just a chance that they got delayed.'

They hadn't been delayed, but they were moving slowly and a ray of hope filtered through the dark clouds of my misery, spurring me on to greater effort. Somewhere near Riden Gaon another request brought the reply I was longing to hear.

'Inglish Expedition maybe one day walking go.'

These words spoken by a smiling farmer charged my failing batteries. Determined to become a member of the expedition I ordered Ang Kami to find another porter, left my rucksack on the farmer's porch, and legged off 'up the Buri', convinced that I could catch them up before nightfall . . .

The path rose and fell like the ECG of a cardiac patient. By the time the daylight drained from the pewter sky, I was entangled in dense undergrowth at a point high above the river where the path climbs steeply through forest up a series of log ladders. Unable to see the trail ahead, unwilling and unable to go back, I sat down in the rain on the muddy path to wait for the morning and ponder the folly of youth.

Fortunately the bite and suck of a plasma of leeches — or whatever their collective noun is — is painless, and either they anaesthetized me or I fainted due to loss of blood, for the long night eventually passed. At dawn, cold, hungry and wet, I clambered through the trees descending steeply towards the river. Heavy with dark water the Buri thundered down its course; a constant roar rising and falling in the echoing confines of its deep gorge. Scrambling over huge slippery boulders where a section of hillside had slumped into the river, I turned a bend and ran slap-bang into the British Himalchuli Expedition camped on a terrace above the river. Soaking, covered with mud, my t-shirt blood-stained from the leech bites, I looked as though I had tangled with the Yeti. Plied with antiseptic by Alastair Stevenson I recounted the epic of Bangladesh, the radios, dysentery and a night in the forest with only vampire leeches for company, by which time everyone was doubled up with laughter and my blood level had been returned to normal with copious cups of *cheeya*. Ang Kami and a porter strolled into camp an hour later, having spent a warm, comfortable night in the farmer's house.

Himalchuli (7,893m/25,895ft), is the southern-most summit of a dramatic trilogy of peaks including Peak 29 (7,835m/25,705ft) and Manaslu (8,118m/26,638ft). Our ambition centred on the unclimbed and unexplored east face of the main peak which is best approached via the Buri Gandaki, a valley at that time closed to trekkers and one that still remains off the beaten track.

The valley of the Buri continued deep and forbidding as the monsoon path scaled its gorge-like flanks beneath an ominous sky. But it was good, at long last, to be part of the 'team', to join in the banter at meal times and feel part of a corporate effort about to climb a mountain. By the time we reached Doban my gut problems had responded to antibiotics, and the discovery of some unexpected hot springs soaked away what remained of my aches and pains. For a while we descended from the high-up monsoon path and followed the true left bank of the river — wading in places along the water's edge where the path was partially submerged — before crossing back to the right bank, after the confluence of the Yaru Khola, to the village of Jagat (1,350m/4,429ft).

Beyond Jagat the path descended an enormous flight of stone steps, overhung in places by a rocky canopy — these led at last to the broad flooded bed of the river. Looking back down the valley, rocky cliffs rose from the river's edge and endless spurs formed a barrier across the river backed by clouds. Our approach up the then rarely visited Buri was taking longer than planned, and the route in the heavy monsoon rain proving much more arduous than we expected. But as we went north it was as if the rains could not penetrate the barrier of the mountains, and each day dawned better than the one before.

After crossing back to the east bank at Gata Khola, we continued in the deepening gorge of the Buri, returning once again by a wooden suspension bridge to the west bank, beyond the confluence of the Chhulung Khola, to climb steeply to the village of Nyak. The steep climb from the river to Nyak brought a change in the vegetation; suddenly we were walking through pine forest and the smell and feel were distinctly Alpine. But any feelings we might have had about this being a Himalayan Switzerland were soon dispelled by the village. With the heavy rain, the street through its centre was awash with liquid manure draining from animal byres below the houses. Our welcome to the village was unfriendly — barking dogs and scowling faces (or were they faeces) greeted our arrival. Our Sirdar, Pemba Tharkay from Phortse, asking permission to camp in a field close to the village, was refused. Instead, as darkness descended, we were told to camp in front of the headman's house on a steaming manure heap!

Shortly after we had pitched our tents a young girl was carried into camp, her left thigh heavily plastered with a poultice of mud and manure. Alastair Stevenson, a dentist by trade and acting expedition doctor, was summoned. Acting as his orderly, we set to, cleaning the oozing mass, aware of the scowling faces, which were critical of the 'round-eyes' magic. Beneath the pus and putrefaction was a gaping dog bite, slicing deep into the muscle. Ill-equipped on the 'shit-heap' to deal with it, nevertheless, we cleaned the tear thoroughly until bright blood flowed and then poured on Savlon and Ciquatrin powder before suturing the wound. As a gesture of gratitude the headman hauled a goat in front of our tent, a lighted taper was put to its beard, and before you could say 'King Charles' a *kukhri* flashed and its head rolled in front of us.

Inside the headman's smoke-filled house, we squatted on the floor and were given bowls of boiled goat and cups of salt tea. The goat whose demise was still fresh in our minds was hard to swallow, whilst the tea — a traditional Tibetan concoction mixed with salt on which floats a scum of rancid butter — looked for all the world like stagnant washing-up water. In the gloom of the smoke-filled room I managed to spirit three bowls of it through a crack in the floor to the animals in the byre below! Elsewhere in Nepal I've enjoyed this brew, but here in Nyak, one of the filthiest villages I've seen and dubbed by the expedition the 'bubonic plague' village, we were all fearful for our health.

West of Nyak, following the course of the Chhulung Khola and leading across the Chhulung Glacier to the Rupina La (4,643m/15,233ft), is a rarely-trekked route, leading south eventually down the Darondi Khola to Ghorka, or alternatively westwards to the Marsyangdi near Uddipur around the southern flank of Baudha Peak (6,672m/ 21,890ft). This would provide an ideal return trip for those wanting to explore the Manaslu/Himalchuli Himals, or the northern side of the Ganesh range via the Shar Khola, without covering old ground. Of course, the ideal circuit would be to trek around the north side of Manaslu, crossing the Larkya La (5,135m/16,847ft) to the Dudh Khola, and joining up with the upper Marsyangdi; alas, this route is closed to trekkers.

Beyond Nyak the culture changes. There are long *mani* walls of intricately-carved stones; mandalas, Lotus flowers and seated Buddhas adorn snaking prayer walls, reflecting the Tibetan origin and Buddhist culture of the upper valley. By the time we reached Namurung the weather had cleared and towering castles of cumulus filled the afternoon sky, replacing the dense grey, wet blanket of the monsoon.

(Opposite) A porter climbs a lethal log ladder through dripping leech-filled forest on the walk up the Buri Gandaki during the monsoon.

Om Mani Padme Om — *the sacred mantra of Buddhist Nepal carved on countless* mani-*stones.*

But now a new storm appeared on the horizon. The villagers of Namurung, a vile-looking bunch misshapen by goitres, refused to let our porters carry through the village, insisting that *they* now carry our loads to Base Camp at double the daily rate of pay. Our Liaison Officer, appointed by the Ministry to sort out local problems, ran off and hid. We had been warned by the Minister in Kathmandu that the people in the upper Buri could be hostile and that many armed Khampa were in the area. Indeed, a previous Japanese expedition had been attacked, and the members were lucky to get away with their lives. In the meantime our loads were being spirited away by the locals and had to be rounded up. In charge of the villagers was a charismatic headman — taller than the others, and handsome, with piercing Rasputin-like eyes. The others, cretinous by comparison, did his bidding. Expecting at any moment to see daggers drawn and our expedition come to an abrupt end, we held a meeting, extraordinary in every way: a council of war.

The way to our Base Camp below the Lidanda Glacier was through and above Namurung. We would obviously have to employ locals. We also

agreed to pay their rates; we had no choice. However, we had to stop the pilfering and in the case of attack we had to defend ourselves. Since I had served some time in the Army and Nigel 'Cookie' Gifford had been in the Catering Corps, and was obviously handy with a filleting knife, we two were called upon to draw up a battle plan. Ice-axes were drawn and each able-bodied member assigned to watch a local.

'John — you should keep an eye on him. Don't let him take his load inside his house.'

'Pin — stay close to the one with the large goitre and make sure he can see you have an ice-axe.'

'Janusz — you can have that evil-looking one with the limp and the shifty eyes.'

'They've all got shifty eyes,' said Alistair.

'But his are more shifty — like a shit-house rat,' quipped John.

Gifford and I would shadow Rasputin. Should things turn 'nasty', we would do an immediate 'Trotsky' on him, which hopefully would quell the uprising. Looking back on it all a decade or so later, I can only assume that Namurung was far higher than the maps made out and that we were all suffering from oxygen starvation! At the time, however, it felt decidedly serious.

Eventually Base Camp was established, although the Namurung bandits refused to carry all the way. But it was a splendid place, set amongst boulders on a moraine below the Lidanda Col. Looking eastwards across the Buri Gandaki Valley, we had splendid views of the Sringi Himal separated from the Ganesh Peaks further to the south by the deep valley of the Shar Khola. Northwards a line of unnamed peaks marked the border with Tibet.

In England we had made the decision to climb the mountain without using high-altitude Sherpas, feeling that effort would be good for us and the result more pure. In reality the way was very long and the climbing tedious, involving huge carries over undulating expanses of glacier before we could even glimpse the objective. But the route was going in well and our supply dump on the Lidanda Col was even visited by something whose footprints were remarkably similar to those photographed by Shipton. I've no idea what or who made them but I'm willing to give it the benefit of the doubt and call it a Yeti — our Sherpas certainly did!

By the time we had established Camp 3 on a high glacier shelf below Rani Peak (6,693m/21,958ft), the mountain still seemed a long way away. Before us was a deep glacier basin into which we would have to descend and cross before the East Face proper could be climbed, and already our communications and supplies seemed thoroughly stretched. Pin and Janusz were fixing a rope down the slope into the basin. I had just arrived at the top of the slope with Gifford, hauling our heavy loads, when the whole of the slope shuddered beneath us and settled again into silence — only the sound of the wind blowing spindrift across the crusty surface remained. Alistair Stevenson had already been carried off in a wind-slab avalanche before Camp 2, fortunately reappearing a hundred yards or so lower down the slope, unhurt! From below two faces appeared on the rope, wide-eyed and white with fear. Late in October a violent storm blasted the mountain; fierce winds armed with icy pellets pelted the tents, all but destroying Camp 2 and trapping two of us at Camp 3. After two days we took advantage of a lull in the blizzard and risked staggering back to Base to lick our wounds and repair our tents.

Back at Base we enjoyed the luxury of rest and a change of clothing, along with Nima Tsering's cooking. Far below on the trail from Namurung we could see a figure lurching towards us. Jokingly the Sherpas cried, 'Yeti Sahib — yeti coming.'

'No — I think it could be Alison,' said Janusz. 'She said that she would come after Annapurna.'

Alison Chadwick was Janusz's wife and a British member of the American Women's Annapurna Expedition, and arguably the strongest and most experienced climber on that expedition. In fact, the figure turned out to be a mail runner. Inside the large dining tent we lounged on foams reading aloud from sections of our mail. Janusz was quiet, staring blankly — unseeing — at his letter.

'What's your news Jan?'

He handed me the sheet of Expedition note paper sent by Arlene Blum, the Annapurna expedition's leader, with its catchy slogan 'A Women's Place is On Top'. It said simply that Alison and her partner Vera had been killed after a fall. Shocked by its contents, I didn't want to believe its message. The letter was read by us all in turn. Janusz went outside into the cold, clear air and inside the turmoil of his mind.

By the morning his plan of action was clear and decisive. He would leave the expedition and go to Annapurna Base Camp to try to recover Alison's body.

It was the death knell of our expedition. My time was running out as my six weeks' leave were coming to an end. For me there would be no time to return to High Camp and push the route forward. Others on the expedition also felt it was time to leave, and with Alison's death a great sadness cloaked the trip.

John, Pin and Alistair still had time, but alone couldn't hope to climb the mountain. Instead they had to be content with an ascent of Rani Peak, an attractive summit above Camp 3.

In the weeks we had been on the mountain, the Buri had altered considerably. The rains had long since finished and the river had resumed a gentler character; much diminished, it was a trickle of its former monsoon self. Now the way south down the valley no longer rose and fell high above the river, but much more often followed its boulder-strewn bed and the gravel banks along its side.

Alastair Stephenson load-hauling on the long moraine above Base Camp leading to Lidanda Col.

On the walk-out a young Gurung boy from Nyak, with marigolds behind his ears,
follows us through 'hell and high water'.

Looking towards the peaks of the Sringi Himal from Base Camp on Himalchuli.

Left empty and dissatisfied with the outcome of the expedition, the return journey for us became a forced march to purge the emotions and to burn the unused energy stored for so long in anticipation of the climb. No longer running with mud, the villages seemed friendlier, with vaguely-remembered smiling faces and children giving the traditional Nepali greeting 'Namaste' ('I salute the god within you'). At Nyak the headman greeted us warmly, and much to my relief his daughter appeared, her thigh healed.

By the time we reached the boulder-strewn valley of the Samrie Khola west of Trisuli, my energy was spent — instead, I had begun to sense the rhythms of Nepal replacing my furious ambition for a summit. More than anything I wanted to stay on to explore other valleys, attempting other peaks. On the rooftop of the bus back to Kathmandu, despite our failure to reach the summit, I made the decision to give up my teaching at Loughborough University and climb professionally; I've rarely regretted it.

ITINERARY:

DAYS 1 – 3: KATHMANDU TO TRISULI (ALLOW 4 TO 6 HOURS BY LOCAL BUS)

Normally takes 2 full days to Arughat bazaar, crossing the Samrie Bhanjyang (1,290m/4,232ft) and the Tharpu Bhanjyang via Katunge bazaar. Arughat is the last opportunity to purchase general supplies. In spring this is a hot walk.

DAYS 4 – 6: ARUGHAT(530m/1,738ft) TO JAGAT (1,350m/4,429ft)

Follow the west bank of the deep Buri Valley. Depending on the season and the rain, take either the riverside or mountain path. There are a few t-houses *en route*. Hot springs near Tatopani. Cross to east bank. The valley widens after Doban. Recross after Lauri to Jagat. Checkpost and store.

DAY 7: JAGAT TO NYAK
(2,300m/7,546ft)
Return to the east bank at Gata Khola, although there is a high path on the west bank. Cross again to the west bank to Chumje and climb to Nyak.

SHAR KHOLA AND THE TOROGOMPA GLACIER
A fine variation, exploring the north side of the Ganesh. This is more difficult than the route up the Buri, but provides superb opportunities to explore a remote and unspoilt valley. The upper Shar Khola is a district called Tzum that unfortunately is out of bounds. Like many areas close to the border, Tibetan Khampa and refugees flooded into Nepal during the 1950s, in this case they crossed the Thaple La from Jongka into the Shar Valley where Milarepa, the Tibetan mystic, is said to have meditated.

From Gata Khola, climb to Philim and follow the path northwards high above the Buri to Ripche in the Shar Khola valley. Continue to Domje. Follow a narrow trail on the north side of the Toromgompa Khola to Chamri Kharka. Time can be spent exploring the glaciers and valleys beneath Ganesh I (7,406m/24,299ft). A return route to Deng north of Nyak is possible on the north side of the Shar Khola via Tumje and Lana. Allow one week for the circuit.

Unfortunately, the route over the Larkya La around the north side of Manaslu remains closed. Namrung (Namru) with its checkpost is the northern limit for trekkers.

RUPINA LA TO GHORKA
West of Nyak the Chhulung Khola offers an alternative return trek to Ghorka, albeit a difficult one requiring basic mountaineering skills to cross the Chhulung Glacier. After the Rupina La the quickest return is down the Dorandi Khola valley to Ghorka. Allow one week.

DIFFICULTY:

The normal route up the Buri Gandaki Valley offers moderately strenuous trekking with plenty of ups and downs but no real altitude. In places the path and the bridges are airy and in wet conditions positively scary. On the other hand, the variations mentioned are much more difficult, requiring basic mountaineering skills and specialist equipment.

LOGISTICS:

There are no sophisticated lodges, and as a result trekkers need to be self-sufficient, although it is nearly always possible to buy some meals in local houses. Local buses run daily between Kathmandu and both Trisuli and Ghorka, taking between 4 and 8 hours. Porters can usually be hired in Trisuli, but would need extra clothing and tents for the Rupina La.

MAPS:

There are no particularly good maps of this area. The Mandala Trekking Map 1:125,000 Kathmandu to Manaslu Ganesh Himal is the best one available.

SEASON:

Go after the monsoon, unless of course you like leeches!

A Campaign of Some Sort:

Around Annapurna

... there in 1950 — weather and the world situation permitting — a campaign of some sort, probably indecisive, ought to take place. 'There' happened to be the Annapurna Himal, because on the map that region seemed to be the most mountainous of a singularly mountainous country.

H.W. Tilman
Nepal Himalaya

Hiking through the foothills and mountains of Nepal must surely rate as one of the most recreational, satisfying and (with caution), healthy pastimes I know. For those who want to explore the physical as well as the human geography of this 'singularly mountainous' kingdom, and delight in its magnificent varied scenery, no trek could better realize these ambitions than a 'circuit' of the Annapurna Himal.

Within Nepal the main Himalayan chain is aligned east to west, the crumpled uplift created by colliding tectonic plates. This magnificent barrier forms a border with Tibet in the north, and is a natural frontier more readily breached by rivers than the arbitrary one that has been created by politicians.

Travelling west from Kathmandu, the Great Himalayan Chain is cleaved first by the Trisuli Gandaki (Bhote Kosi), and again on the western side of the Ganesh Himal by the Buri Gandaki, which in my experience proves the most difficult of trans-Himalayan valleys to follow. By the time you reach the ancient fortress town of Gorkha, another great valley — the Marsyangdi Khola — cuts a cleft through the mountains, forming the eastern limit of the Annapurnas, separating them from a trilogy of giants — Manaslu (8,151m/26,742ft), Peak 29 (7,835m/25,705ft) and Himalchuli (7,893m/25,896ft). The western boundary of the Annapurna Himal, some forty miles away, is defined by the impressive defile of the Kali Gandaki. This flows south from the arid landscape of 'forbidden' Mustang, between the giants of Dhaulagiri 1 (8,167m/26,795ft) and Annapurna 1 (8,091m/26,545ft), creating the deepest river valley in the world.

Within the serried summits of the Annapurna Himal are twelve mountains greater than 7,000m (22,960ft) and a host of other peaks over 6,000m (19,680ft). Within a year of Nepal opening up to Western mountaineers, all but the southern boundary of the Annapurnas had been traced. A French expedition, under the leadership of Maurice Herzog, followed the course of the Kali Gandaki looking for a route to Dhaulagiri, but found instead costly success on Annapurna 1. In so doing, their quest for a possible route to Annapurna led them over the Tilicho Passes to the upper reaches of the Marsyangdi and Manang. They also traced what was already a traditional route over the Thorong La (5,240m/17,200ft), connecting Manang with Muktinath. A few weeks after the French had descended on the Manangba, a British

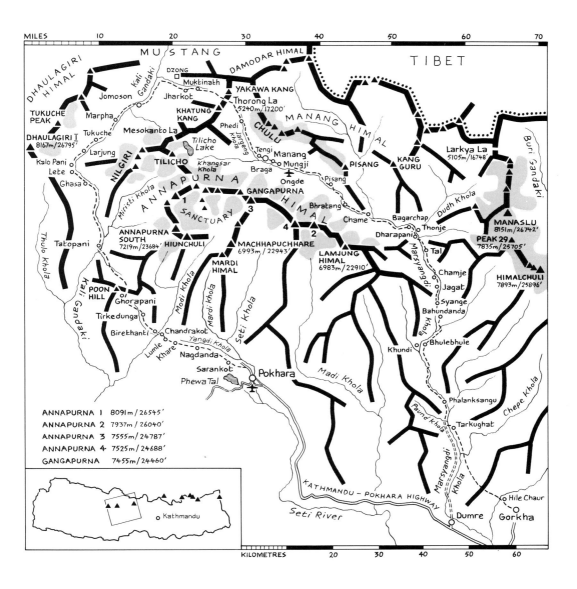

ANNAPURNA 1   8091m / 26545'
ANNAPURNA 2   7937m / 26040'
ANNAPURNA 3   7555m / 24787'
ANNAPURNA 4   7525m / 24688'
GANGAPURNA   7455m / 24460'

expedition led by the ubiquitous Tilman was also on the doorstep, having followed the course of the Marsyangdi Khola. The Chinese invasion of Tibet and its subsequent occupation, combined with the closing of Nepal to tourism in the 1960s, meant that the area was once again off-limits to Western adventurers. By 1970, trekking along the Kali was possible but it was not until 1977 that Manang, along with the Thorong La, were re-opened and a 'Circuit of the Annapurnas' possible.

We had driven from Kathmandu taking five hard hours in a smoke-spewing bus to reach Gorkha (1,219m/4,000ft), the ancient seat of Prithvinarayan Shah. It was from this expansive town (named after the hermit and saint Gorkhanath), that the head of the house of Gorkha, Prithvinarayan Shah, and a powerful army subdued the valley of Kathmandu, and succeeded in uniting Nepal in prolonged campaigns between 1744–1769.

Despite the altitude, the midday heat was stifling, and the climb from the bazaar up stone steps to the ancient palace, which is close to the hermit's cave, proved a great effort. With little time left of the day we hiked westwards down a pleasant wooded ridge to our tents, pitched by the river at Hile Chaur.

By taking this route from Gorkha, rather than driving the new bulldozed road up the main valley to Phalanksangu, we extended our trek by three days. But opting for the pedestrian route meant that we were able to enjoy some delightful walking through intricately-terraced fields and mango groves, before joining the main thoroughfare across the river south of Thakughat (580m/1900ft).

Having lost altitude, we now sweltered up the open road, cursing passing trucks and the swirling dust devils they created that caked our sweaty faces to a dirty dough. Having chewed grit for an hour or so, we found cool relief in the Paund Khola, when we shared a deep pool with bemused buffaloes and giggling village girls who pounded washing on smooth stones. Sallie, my wife, drying off beside the stream, jumped back in alarm when a flying hiss of a snake and a rikki-tikki chattering mongoose in hot pursuit brushed against her legs in their chase through the rustling grass.

The heat in the valley was oppressive and our bodies, not yet acclimatized to the sub-tropical conditions, were prickly with sweat. In Phalanksangu we bartered for flip-flops and umbrellas before crossing the bridge and hiking

northwards through numerous villages towards cloud-covered mountains. One of the problems with the trek up both the Marsyangdi and the Kali Gandaki is that you gain little altitude until quite close to the Thorong La — the final climb comes as a nasty shock to those that haven't spent time acclimatizing before the crossing.

An unforgettable highlight in the Marsyangdi beyond Bhulebhule are countless fine falls that plunge as transparent shrouds or silky threads of light down verdant cliffs. We couldn't resist the temptation to bathe in several of the deep, rock-filled splash-pools hidden at their base.

On the steep climb towards Bahundanda, a line of sure-footed ponies descended past us, one of several we were to meet on the 'circuit'. Unshod, each had a traditional patterned saddle rug and wood *kangtaga* (saddle), with a plumed headdress and bridle of bells. Like the porters of Nepal, they have hard, sinewy bodies, and the fibres of their well-defined muscles flex beneath thin revealing skin under loads of wool or salt. They seem, man and animals alike, to be anatomical models, or Old Master drawings made animate. Unstoppable, their hoof-fall made a constant ringing clip clop down the stone steps as they filed their relentless way towards Gorkha. Only the pungent smell of sweat and dung remained up the trail, long after their bells were silent.

Meetings like this and time spent in local houses or villages are the real rewards of trekking these trade routes. Despite the changes that 'progress' and exposure to other cultures will inevitably bring about, Nepal, because of its material poverty and geographical limitations, is locked in a medieval time-warp where few people or things seem greatly affected. In any case they are not museum exhibits and it is we who have to be careful not to become 'precious' about preserving 'quaint cultures' for our amusement rather than their benefit.

Having crossed to the west bank of the river

we trekked northwards through an increasingly impressive gorge, passing under beetling overhangs until the settlement of Jagat. Yet another string of ponies were a reminder of the ancient salt trade with Tibet and this town's importance as a checkpost.

From Chamje (1,433m/4,700ft) the valley's character once again alters. Passing between the portals of Lamjung Himal (6,983m/22,910ft) and Peak 29 (7,835m/25,705ft), we climbed high above the river, through a narrow pass, beyond which a perfectly flat silt and gravel bed filled the classical 'U' shape of the valley. In the middle of this flush floor, which was once a lakebed, is the small community of Tal (1,707m/5,600ft).

In a country where, thankfully, very little is flat, these level meadows seem merely to emphasise the impressive verticality of the rest. We strolled up the main street, stopping at a lodge where a horse was hitched to a rail. There were no swing doors to a saloon bar, but instead we sat on the porch drinking beers watching the world go by. Tal definitely felt like a one-horse Wild West town. Our Sherpas, especially the Sirdar Ang Zambo, had gauged the feeling and marshalled a string of hardy ponies for some sport. In a grassy pasture around our campsite, which was between two stunning waterfalls behind the town, we staged the 'wacky races'. The 'sherps' sat well but not easily astride the small mustangs, whilst we lanky 'round-eyes' literally ploughed furrows with our feet as we raced bareback across the flat. In the end even the porters, who had looked on in shocked horror, joined in the fun. We finally retired to our tents with our ribs aching from laughter, and sore for the want of a saddle.

Between Manaslu and Lamjung Himal, the sun entered the gorge late, long after we had

Crossing a traditional vine and twig bridge over the Marsyangdi River.

Peaks of the Annapurna Himal seen from the rhododendron-clad slopes of the Poon Hill Danda above Ghorapani Deorali.

hiked beneath high, hanging valleys and delicate waterfalls to cross the bridge below Dharapani (1,943m/6,375ft). On the far side of the river the narrow canyon of the Dudh Khola opens a way to the north-east and the Larkya La (5,105m/16,748ft), which leads around the north side of Manaslu into the valley of the Buri Gandaki. In 1978 I was a member of a British Expedition to the East Face of Himalchuli and at the time would have loved to have walked out from the mountain over this pass. But then it wasn't possible for me and now for trekking parties the route is still out of bounds. It remains one of the anomalies in Nepal that expeditions can get permission to trek to their Base Camp through areas that are closed to trekking groups.

Shortly after Dharapani the valley swings westwards behind the Lamjung Himal and the bulk of the Annapurnas, carving between the Great Himalayan Crest, and the Damodar and Manang Himals that make up the Ladakh Lekh to the north. By the time we reached Bagarchap, the architecture had changed to stone buildings with flat roofs, resembling much more closely those of Tibet than those of lower Nepal. We camped nearby, opposite a small hot spring flowing into the cold waters of the Marsyangdi; a marvellous cure was provided for aching muscles and sweaty bodies.

Despite the fact that the upper Marsyangdi is in the rain-shadow of the Annapurnas and is known as an arid region, it was raining hard — but perhaps I have the meaning wrong? By midday we had had enough of walking through icy rain beneath a canopy of dark pines, so I

(Opposite) A highlight of the Marsyangdi trek — 'countless fine waterfalls that plunge as transparent shrouds and silky threads down verdant cliffs'. This one is near Tal.

called a halt at a *bhatti* near Tanzo, Inside, the main room was dark, unlit except by smoky light filtering through gaps in the rafters and the low door. We crammed inside, sitting on the mud floor around a small fire, and ordered *chai* — hot, sweet and milky. Slowly my eyes got used to the dim light, but not to the smoke which made them water and my nose run. On the earth, in front of the open fire, a grimy, swollen-bellied infant wearing a tea-cosy hat and tattered vest crawled towards the embers. Just as he neared incineration an elder sister took him by the ankles and dragged him, laughing, to safety, through mud of his own making.

By the time we reached Bhratang, having passed through the police checkpost at Chame, we had been trekking for over a week and were looking forward to reaching Nyesyang District. This is the high arid region of Manang north of the Annapurna Himal, where customs and dress, as well as much of the landscape, have close kinship with Tibet. Just beyond the town, as I climbed with Sallie towards Pisang, we had a sharp reminder of the *khampas* (Tibetan warrior/bandits), once strong in the area. Walking along a forest trail that felt very Alpine, we entered a clearing with a small *mani* wall. As we returned to look back down the valley at the enormous glaciated rock slabs above Talung, wet and glistening under a fresh fall of snow, two wild-eyed horsemen charged down the path through the pines. Dressed in skins and ear-flap hats, one wore a heavy turquoise earring, and the other, with braided plaits, sported a gold tooth. They were trailing a third pony with saddle-bags draped across a fine blanket, and it seemed to me that they were at least making off the with spoils of war or the ill-gotten gain from highway robbery. In fact, they were quite possibly simple inn keepers from a trekkers' lodge in Manang!

But the Manangba are never quite what they seem. I was squatting in an unadorned *bhatti* in Pisang, talking to the woman spooning sugar into boiling tea with hard hands. Her dirty clothes and cast-off trainers belied the fact that she and many Manangba have a long-established tradition as traders, and are far from being poor *bhotes*, as the large chunks of dark coral and exquisite turquoise in her necklace proved. Their trade is not simply between Tibet and lower Nepal, in the way that Sherpas are the 'highland traders' in the east, but they act as middlemen in international import and export carried on between Nepal and the Far East. Their merchandise goes beyond simple staples and is reputed to involve black market dealings in gold and currency! This trade has its origins in a dispensation granted by the King almost 200 years ago, allowing the Manangba passports and the right to trade abroad.

From a camp near the STOL airstrip at Ongde we explored the valley towards Annapurna 4 (7,525m/24,688ft), climbing to a sharp moraine crest for a better look at Annapurna 3 (7,555m/24,787ft), and the Chulu Peaks opposite. On the northern side of the valley there are several peaks, included on the trekking peak list, that offer some good climbing.

Despite the recent rain (which above Pisang fell as snow), the landscape shows all the signs of being in the shadow of the Annapurnas. What trees there are tend to be sparse, covering pockets of dry hillside with birch, pine, juniper and scrubby rhododendron. In places tamarind and berberis add a touch of colour to a landscape of crumbling organ pipes weathered from wind-blown moraines.

After calling on the HRA post at Ongde we hiked towards Manang. Crossing the river near Munji we soon entered Braga. Strongly Tibetan in style, Braga's houses perch on platforms up the steep hillside looking like a fortress against a backcloth of moraine cliffs, carved into fantasy castles with turrets and spires around which black choughs soar. Walking between the houses, up narrow allies connecting rooftop with veranda, we climbed to the ancient *gompa* which looks out over the valley from a terrace of fluttering prayer flags. Finding the door bolted, we began to descend, when an old rogue, who looked even older than the monastery, appeared with a bunch of keys, the largest of which was rammed into the ancient lock. Our 'guide' now showed us the intriguing interior with its endless row of saints, the Buddhist pantheon made up of 108 terracotta statues. Telling us that these dust-laden images were over two million years old, he pointed out that he had many genuine Buddha relics and that they were expensive to maintain (wink-wink, nudge-nudge). This commentary came from a mouth containing blackened tombstone teeth that looked older than the saints themselves. In fact the *gompa* is old – 500 years is the informed estimate.

An hour or so beyond Braga is Manang (3,351m/10,994ft), the largest community in the valley. Built on a river terrace above the valley floor, its stone houses cling together, roof and terrace contiguous, as one rises from another, linked by notched-log ladders. Between the buildings, narrow ginnels with intricate prayer wheels and covered arches provide a maze down which to wander, giving stunning glimpses of Gangapurna (7,455m/24,460ft) and Annapurna 3 (7,555m/24,787ft) across the valley. From the combined catchment of Gangapurna and Tarke Kang, a tongue of cascading ice extends towards Manang. From its mouth dribbling melt-water has collected to form a moraine-dammed lake around which prayer flags flutter.

As we left the town, climbing past long *mani* walls towards Tengi, we met a group of trekkers retreating from the Thorong La. The snow and rain of the last week had made their crossing of the pass impossible, dressed as they were in light trekking clothes. Sensibly, after spending a couple of nights in the dingy *bhatti* at Thorong Phedi, they had decided to go down. The route to the frozen Tilicho Lake that crosses the Mesokanto La follows the Khangsar Khola, north-west from here, passing beneath the

An old woman in Braga climbs the hill towards the gompa, *carrying a traditional Tibetan salt or butter tea churn.*

Great Barrier of Annapurna. In better conditions this provides a magnificent, albeit more difficult, alternative to the Thorong route. We now traversed high above the Jargeng Khola northwards, beneath the impressive south face of Chulu West and Central, before a narrowing valley led to the cul-de-sac at Phedi below the pass.

It was a cold camp and the porters appreciated the extra warm clothing they were issued. Thankfully we were a strong party and well equipped as we left in darkness, kicking steps up the frozen scree between rock cliffs to gain a snow-covered notch. There was no trace of a path, but Ang Zambo knew the route and etched a perfect line up and around snow-covered moraine. Trail-breaking through deep snow,

99

Seen from the trail to the Thorong La the flat-roofed dwellings of Manang are built on a terrace above the juvenile Marsyangdi, and overlooked by the soaring north flank of Annapurna 2 (7,937m/26,040ft).

with only the odd cairn as a guide, was exhausting work. Shortly after sunrise we crashed on the beautiful snow-covered crest of the pass between the icy peaks of Khatung Kang (6,484m/21,273ft) and Yakawa Kang (6,482m/22,398ft), counting everyone through before pressing on.

Descending westwards towards the valley of the Jhang Khola, we soon left the snow behind and gained an ever-widening landscape of massive mountains beyond the Kali Gandaki. By the time we reached the sacred poplar grove at Muktinath we had descended nearly five and a half thousand cartilage-crushing feet. Within this spinney is a cluster of temples, amongst the most sacred Hindu sites of pilgrimage. Enshrined in one of the temples, called Jwala Mai, natural gas causes flames to flicker on water, soil and rock, although when I last looked below the altar those on the stone had gone out.

Apart from a couple of holy men tending the flames, the grove was empty — despite the state of disrepair of some of the buildings, it has an unearthly atmosphere.

Losing height quickly, the path passes the town of Jharkot (3,612m/11,850ft), a Tibetan-style fortified settlement. Now both the weather and landscape changed. Beneath a deep blue sky we looked across the arid Jhang Valley to a ruined *dzong* (fortress), once the palace of the local ruler, and north-westwards to the dry moonscape of Mustang, part of the Forbidden Kingdom.

Jomosom or Dzong Sam (2,713m/8,000ft) was easily reached in the day from Muktinath, even though we scoured the shingle banks of the Kali's flood plain for ammonites, and enjoyed the bustle and activity of lines of ponies commuting along the valley trading route.

During the late afternoon the Nilgiri Peaks,

north, south and central, reflected the sun like polished steel, whilst we struggled against a rising wind that howled down the corridor of the valley. Armed with sand and grit from the dry river bed, it blasted our already sunburned cheeks and was our constant companion for two more days. Between Jomosom and Kalo Pani (2,530m/8,300ft), where the river flows between the Dhaulagiri and Annapurna giants, there is over 5,400m (18,000ft) between the summits and the valley floor. The villagers along here are mostly Thakali, although one sees a great many Tibetan-looking characters trading out of Mustang. Many settlements have high walls built around a central courtyard, no doubt as protection from the constant wind.

The character of the trekking in this valley feels quite different; although it is much less rugged than the Marsyangdi, its scale is more impressive. It is a much more travelled route, and we passed other trekkers coming from Pokhara, making use of the many sophisticated lodges that have spring up along the way. At Jomosom, Marpha and Tukuche we met multi-national cliques of trekkers, 'hanging out' at comfortable Thakali-run *bhattis*, their heads buried in earnest books and exotic tobacco in search of karma and salvation on the road to Muktinath.

South from Lete (2,438m/7,999ft) the nature of the gorge changes. The path becomes narrower, wetter and even deeper, and in places is carved into the steep cliff-face. When you are walking along these precipitous tunnels, the open outer wall provides a giddy spectacle of the thundering river far below. In places you can see signs of older paths cut in the cliff above the present high-level route, and also holes for the wooden stakes that formed horizontal walkways jutting out from vertical cliffs. These hazardous trails have been used by pilgrims and traders for over two thousand years. In 1978 I traversed an

A beautiful Gurung woman and child. The ethnic diversity around Annapurna is as varied as the trekking itself.

identical gantry in the Buri Gandaki and was very impressed!

Tatopani (1,219m/3,999ft), below the confluence of the Miristi Khola and Kali, gets its name from the hot springs found on either side of the river. Over the years that I've been visiting it there has been much development. The Thakali inhabitants are making the most of the boom in tourism to develop lodges and stores. Trendy Western-style cafés and cake shops have opened up, and even the hot springs have been turned into a Nepali version of a public baths. In conjunction with the Annapurna Conservation Area Project (ACAP), experiments in energy generation and conservation are taking place here (as elsewhere in an area of 2,600 square kilometres covering the Annapurna Circuit). Hopefully, it will provide, in 1,000 square miles, a relevant model of ecological development that is both harmonious to tourism and environmental protection. With 96 per cent of Nepal's energy coming from wood, the forests are disappearing at an annual rate of 3 per cent and it has been estimated that a busy lodge can burn one hectare of rhododendron forest yearly to meet the demands of trekkers. I believe that ACAP, with its alternative, low-technology approach, will allow local inhabitants to prosper in the long term without destroying the environment that travellers come to see. I would exhort everyone visiting the Annapurnas to abide by ACAP's 'Minimum Impact Code', which applies equally all over Nepal.

The good news about the hike to Ghorapani (GhoDapani) is that it gets you out of the valley and opens up the horizon. The bad news is that you have to 'bust a gut' to do it, reminding me of Christina Rossetti's poem, *Up Hill*:

> *Does the road wind up-hill all the way?*
> > *Yes, to the very end.*
> *Will the day's journey take the whole long day?*
> > *From morn till night my friend.*
>
> *But is there for the night a resting place?*
> > *A roof for when the slow dark hours begin?*
> *May not the darkness hide it from my face?*
> > *You cannot miss that inn.*

As you approach the Kali Gandaki from Muktinath, the town of Jharkot stands like a ruined Tibetan dzong against the Dhaula Himal.

Over 1,500m (5,000ft) of unbroken uphill hiking following the flank of the Ghara river to the *deorali* (pass) form the watershed between the Ghara and Bhurungdi Kholas. But *what* a hike — soon after crossing the second suspension bridge, you climb through terraced fields where there are splendid views northwards towards Nilgiri South (6,839m/22,438ft), rising above the heavily-wooded Miristi Khola. Frequent *chautaara* ease the haul and offer an opporunity to rest and marvel at the vision of Dhaulagiri and distant Tukuche Peak, framed by the shadowy boughs of a *bhanyan* tree. Beyond the terraces, pasture and stands of rhododendron mottle the hillside that leads to the growing cluster of lodges that saddle the pass (2,834m/9,298ft).

Poon Hill (3,198m/10,491ft), rising to the west of the col, is justifiably one of the most famous viewpoints in Nepal. It looks out across the Kali Gandaki towards the Dhaulagiri Himal, but also takes in the Annapurnas and Machhapuchhare. At dawn, when the sun rises over the shoulder of the 'Fish-Tail', it strikes first on the magnificent southern flank of Dhaulagiri towering above the purple depths of the Kali's Gorge.

Our time on trek was running out, leaving only enough to descend down the valley to Birethanti. From the summit of Poon Hill I had noticed a sinuous ridge snaking south, parallel with the Kali Gandaki, and appearing, on the map at least, to terminate at its confluence with the Modi Khola. This unknown, untracked gem would have to brood until another year. Descending at first through Tolkienesque woods of gnarled oaks and rhododendrons, and later down an interminable stairway of stone steps, we passed herds of pack ponies making the upward climb. From the bridge over the Modi Khola at Birethanti (1,097m/3,399ft) there is a final short sharp climb to Chandrakot (1,563m/5,128ft) and Khare (1,646m/5,400ft), before moving along the Kaski Danda towards Nagdanda (1,425m/4,675ft), where there is the magnificent final panorama of the Annapurna massif around which you have just trekked. By the time we had descended to Phedi and walked out through parched paddy fields and the Tibetan Refugee Camp back to Pokhara, we had been on the trail for over three weeks. By the most conservative estimate we had covered a glorious one hundred and fifty mountainous miles, leaving no doubt in my mind that this classic circuit is one of the greatest walks in the mountain world.

ITINERARY:

DAYS 1 – 3: KATHMANDU TO PHALANKSANGU

Bus from Kathmandu to Gorkha (4 – 6 hours). Follow wooded ridge north-west to Santipipal and Hile Chaur. Into Darondi Khola Valley and climb to Luitel Bhanjyang (700m/2,300ft). Hot walking. Descend into Marsyangdi Valley. Level walking, join road at Tarkughat. Follow this to Phalanksangu. It is possible to travel by road from Dumre, eliminating 2 days.

DAYS 4 – 5: PHALANKSANGU TO SYANGE (1,067m/3,500ft)

Cross bridge leaving road to continue up true right bank to Bensisahar. Stay on true left bank through Ampchaur and Simalchaur. Good views of Lamjung Himal and Namun Bhanjyang, an interesting and difficult variation into Manang from Pokhara. Continue through numerous Gurung villages to Bhulebhule (shops). Impressive waterfalls begin. Well-engineered trail to Syange, the northern limit of rice cultivation.

Sallie O'Connor on the descent from the Thorong La, looking across the arid landscape near Muktinath and the Kali Gandaki to the eastern end of the Dhaula Himal.

DAYS 6–7: SYANGE TO CHAME

Valley changes character. More rugged to Gadi Jagat, and more waterfalls. Cross suspension bridge to reach drained lake flats at Tal. Continue on east bank recrossing river to Dharapani. Interesting side trip to Tamung meadows, but allow two days. Continue to Bagarchap (2,713m/8,625ft). More Tibetan in character with stone houses and *mani*. Hot springs. Continue on south side of river to Chame (2,713m/8,625ft), the administrative centre for the district. Checkpost, bank and *gompa*.

DAYS 8 – 9: CHAME TO MANANG:

Main valley swings north-west. Walk through pine glades to Taleku. Spectacular waterfalls. Cross covered bridge to Khampa settlement of Bhratang (2,919m/9,575ft). Continue to Pisang. Stay on south side of river to Ongde. STOL airstrip and HRE post. Cross river to Braga village with its fine *gompa*. Continue to Manang.

Note: Before going higher you are advised to spend a couple of days acclimatizing before crossing the Thorong La.

DAY 10: MANANG TO THORONG PHEDI

There are now some small lodges on the way, should you want to break the journey.

DAY 11: PHEDI TO MUKTINATH

Pre-dawn start to a long day. Stiff climb to a snow-covered Thorong La (5,240m/17,200ft) with a long descent to Muktinath. Sometimes there are t-shops open on the way. The crossing should only be attempted in good conditions. Porters must be properly equipped.

DAY 12: MUKTINATH TO JOMOSOM

Fine views of Dhaulagiri and north towards dusty Mustang. Past ruins of Jharkot — worth a visit. Descend into Kali Gandaki. Continue in windy valley to Jomosom. STOL airstrip. Clinic.

DAYS 13 – 16: JOMOSOM TO TATOPANI

Spectacular walking through world's deepest valley. Busy trans-Himalayan trade route, between Pokhara and Mustang. Interesting side trips to Dhaulagiri icefall and Annapurna north side Base Camp. Tatopani, large town with hot springs.

DAY 17: TATOPANI TO GHORAPANI

A mammoth (1,500m/5,000ft) climb. Spectacular views. Plenty of campsites and the odd *bhatti*. Poon Hill is a must at dawn or dusk.

DAYS 18 – 21: GHORAPANI TO POKHARA

Most scenic route is via Ghandrung to the Modi Khola with a long climb to Landrung. Continue via Beri Kharka and a long descent to Phedi. Vehicle transport then possible to Pokhara or you can walk via Hyenja and Tibetan refugee camp to Pokhara.

DIFFICULTY:

Apart from one or two climbs this is a moderate trek, although there are plenty of ups and downs in the 150-mile circuit. Thorong La is the highest point on the trek and requires adequate warm and windproof clothing for trekkers and porters alike. It is of course possible to do the trek in the other direction, making the ascent to Thorong La almost 915m (3,000ft) longer!

LOGISTICS:

Buses run daily between Kathmandu and Gorkha. From Dumre it is possible to drive to Phalanksangu. Porters can be hired in Gorkha. There are plenty of lodges around the circuit, although the one at Phedi is simple and often crowded. Those in the Kali are very sophisticated. The area is part of the Annapurna Conservation Project so those camping need to carry and use paraffin.

MAPS:

Generally poor. The Mandala Trekking Map, Pokhara to Jomosom Manang Sheet 1:125,000, is the best available.

SEASON:

Post-monsoon tends to be the most reliable time for the trek. May and early April, although good for flowers, are bad for snow — the pass might prove impossible.

The Other Nepal:
Rafting to the Terai to encounter tiger and Tharus

*There's a one-eyed yellow idol to the north of
    Kathmandu,*
There's a little marble cross below the town;
*There's a broken-hearted woman tends the grave of
    Mad Carew,*
And the Yellow God forever gazes down.

J. Milton Hayes

For most travellers, a journey to Nepal fulfils the dream of trekking in the Himalaya, or at least in the crumpled landscape that forms the hills at the foot of the eternal snows. Quickly out of Kathmandu their eyes look northwards, trying to recognise Everest, Annapurna, Manaslu or Langtang. At Tribhuvan, the capital's international airport, it's easy to 'spot the trekker' or mountaineer, struggling overladen from the aircraft in an attempt to get through with their excess baggage. Wearing the bulky things they couldn't stuff into allowed luggage, they waddle through the customs hall dressed in mountain boots, down parkas and heavy sweaters — better equipped for Base Camp than Kathmandu.

Those first few days in the kingdom are always a heady affair. Spaced-out on jetlag and airline fast food, the mystical atmosphere of this fabulous city acts like a narcotic as I wander along its crowded alleys, feeling the fabric of the place. It bustles with a hectic, social street life and trade, interwoven with the deities of Buddhist, Hindu and Animistic faiths, as much

a part of the Nepali's daily life as rice and water. Things magical to the Westerner mingle with the mundane in Nepal, echoing Kipling:

*Still the world is wondrous large
    Seven seas from marge to marge —
And it holds a various kinds of man,
    And the wildest dreams of Kew*

*Are the facts of Kathmandu
    And the crimes of Clapham
Chaste at Martaban*

At the end of six weeks' hard climbing in Ganesh I had less meat on my bones than a butcher's apron. The walk-out down the airy Tiru Danda had sliced through the middle hills like a sabre-cut, but I was physically tired and needed a change of scene before leaving on another trek that would take me back to the Jugal Himal.

With time to spare in the city I was doing the rounds of the restaurants — breakfast in the garden of the Pumpernickel, followed by lunch at KC's, or tea and stickies at the Annapurna Coffee Shop, head buried in a book or a bun. This isn't, as most first-time travellers to Nepal would assume, a recipe for Kathmandu Quickstep or Delhi Belly, because there are countless first-rate bolt holes where gourmet and *gourmand* alike can satiate culinary cravings cultivated on trek.

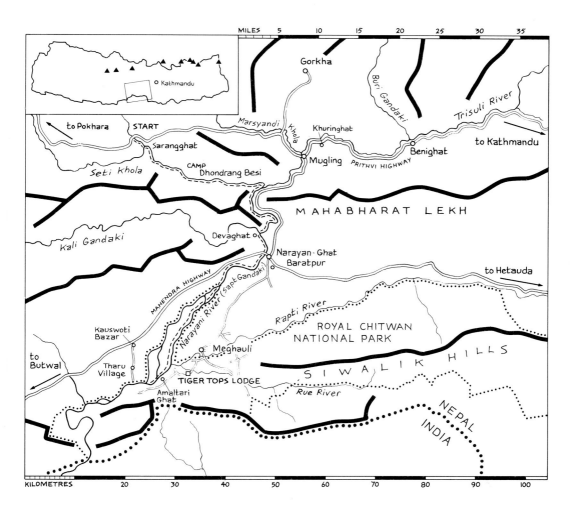

'You look positively wasted.'

These words of encouragement came from Lisa Van Gruisen, a long-time friend and resident of Kathmandu, during dinner at the Ghar e Kebab. In the background the essence of the sub-continent was being captured by the interwoven rhythms of an evening *rarg* played on sitar and tamboor, far removed from the cold high glacier camps of little over a week before.

'You obviously need a change of scene — your eyes have the empty stare of Mad Carew — before you go off in search of the "green-eyed yellow idol" why don't you go down to Chitwan and "shoot" a few tiger? We need some photographs for the new brochure.'

By the time the cardamom tea was poured it had all been planned. The lady had said, 'Go south, young man.' So I did.

If you traverse Nepal from north to south it is possible to divide the country into at least seven major geological zones. The northernmost zone covers those mountains on the edge of the Tibetan Plateau, beyond the Greater Himalaya that, in West Nepal, north of Dhaulagiri and the Annapurnas, form the border with Tibet. Between these mountains and the Himalaya proper is a line of east-west-running valleys that have eroded the softer sedimentary rocks between the harder granites and gneiss of the mountain ranges. This feature is well seen in Manang and the upper Marsyangdi *en route* to the Thorong La. South of this are the Greater Himalaya, made up of the world's highest mountains. South of and parallel to the mountains are the foothills of the Himalaya. These are a complicated washboard of undulating ridges and steep-sided valleys, carved by mighty rivers that flow from the glaciers and snows of the mountains. A few of these rivers have their sources in Tibet, transecting the Tibetan ranges and the Himalaya as the action of down-cutting has kept pace with mountain uplift. These provide the great trans-Himalayan trade routes. South of this complicated heartland are two ranges of mountains and hills — the Mahabharat Lekh and the Siwaliks — and beyond these the Terai, a dramatic contrast to the crumpled hills. This is an extension of the Ganges Plain, a low-lying area of sand and gravel dissected by meandering shallow rivers and streams that change their channels with the seasons. It is also the location of the Royal Chitwan National Park, a forested valley drained by the Rapti River.

There are several ways for the traveller to get to the Terai and Chitwan, a wildlife preserve that was once the hunting reserve for the kingdom's rulers. In 1911, King George V hunted in Chitwan. His hunting party of 2,000 attendants and 600 elephants had a following of 12,000. At the end of a five-day *shikar*, when the place must have been trampled flat, the kill included 58 tigers, 28 rhino, half a dozen sloth bears and enough deer to feed an army. A short flight takes you quickly to Meghauli, or else the road provides a tedious jolting journey to the jungle. But by far the most adventurous and romantic route is to ride the white water of the Trisuli and Seti rivers south, through the middle hills to the very edge of the preserve.

Many Himalayan rivers are ideally suited to rafting. Once beyond the impractical upper reaches, they become, in the middle course of their journey through the foothills, spectacular white-water rivers. For most of the year they have high volumes of water, providing every kind of 'fun-run', for expert and novice alike. On the river I was going to ride, the Seti Khola, technical difficulty, danger and white-water thrills were not the major assets for me, although it does have some exciting rapids spread along its course. Rather, the real joy of the journey would be found in making a traverse; taking a geological cross-section, from the Midlands of Nepal, the cultural heartland of the country that in places is 90km (60 miles) wide and between 600 and 2,000m (1,970–6,560ft) high, to the Terai and the Gangetic Plain. South of the Himalaya many principal rivers furrow the Midlands, including the Tamur, Arun, Sun Khosi, Trisuli, Kali Gandaki Beri, Karnali, Seti and Chamlia, continuing south through the Mahabharat Lekh, a mountain chain that has acted like a natural fortification to protect the heartland through the ages against invasion from the south. These heavily-forested metamorphic mountains provide only marginal farmland created in forest clearings on steeply terraced hillsides. South of the Mahabharat Lekh the final folded foothills of Nepal are found in the Siwaliks, whose tertiary rocks of alternating soft and resistant strata form the terminal wrinkles of the Himalayan orogenesis. The Siwaliks end dramatically in the Terai, a forested flood plain of alluvium less than 200m (650ft) above sea level. Once a Sal and oak forest, and the home of the sub-continent's elusive wildlife, much of it has been settled and cleared and the once endemic malaria all but eliminated. What remains of the natural environment is preserved as the Royal Chitwan National Park. Concentrated within the park's 60 by 100km (40 by 67 miles) boundary, and encroached on by

The boatman fights to hold his line as the raft bucks and bends like a stallion trying to throw its rider . . . On the Seti River.

settlements and farmland, can be found Bengal tigers, leopards, sloth bears, one-horned rhino, and a multitude of deer and antelope, whilst in the rivers are gharhial, marsh-mugger crocodile and the rarely-seen Gangetic dolphin. The forest and rivers, as well as the cats, mammals and reptiles, provides an ornithologist's paradise with over 250 species of birds.

As promised, Lisa had organized the whole thing.

'Leave it to me — just be ready at six tomorrow morning. We have a raft going down to Tiger Tops and I'm sure they have room for one more.'

Right on cue the transport arrived at the Guest House in Thamel where I was staying, and before I could rustle up breakfast we were jolting along the Pokhara Road *en route* for the Seti River. My companions were a friendly bunch, doing Nepal virtually from end to end in two travel-packed weeks that included a short

trek out of Pokhara, white-water rafting and a Chitwan safari, as well as sightseeing in Kathmandu. Busy, professional people, they obviously engaged in 'power-travelling' along with power-breakfasts and power-dressing!

At the put-in the boatmen were waiting. The three rafts had already been inflated and the inevitable horde of curious children had gathered to witness the spectacle. We struggled to pack valuables in rubber bags and cameras in watertight ammunition boxes. As we went through safety procedures and put on life-jackets on the bank, we looked an unlikely crew — Nepali boatmen trained on the Colorado, a weary mountaineer and an assortment of middle-aged businessmen and their wives. I could sense that they were more than a little apprehensive about the thrills and possible spills into rapids, and about the quality of Nepali water; which they had been conditioned not to touch. As one of the group pointed out, 'Apart from all those Nepalis washing in it, putting their dead into it and crapping into it, fish make love in it!' Added to these problems of course was the possibility of a close encounter with a suitably-named marsh-mugger croc.

Once we were afloat, the water's flow pulled us into the winding 'V' of the Seti's valley, and we meandered through the heavily-forested hills of the Mahabharat Lekh. Between the excitement of the rapids we floated silently with the fast flow of the deep green water. Bird song was a constant accompaniment to silence, as were the curious stares of monkeys collecting berries along the water's edge.

Then a distant roar, quiet at first, would herald the next rapid, growing louder as the boatmen pulled on the oars and used the current to hold a good position in the quickening flow. Ahead, the river was stepped — the water ended and dropped over an edge marked by a white-water plume of a standing wave.

Spinning the rubber raft so as to face downstream, our boatmen hold a line between two half-hidden rocks where the river is channelled in a black 'V' over the fall. In the bow of the boat I brace against its tubular side in anticipation of the ride, holding on to a rein of rope like a rodeo cowboy in the stocks. I feel the raft accelerate as it is sucked into the maelstrom of frantic roaring water, and it bucks and bends like a newly-mounted stallion trying to spill its rider. Pushed towards a massive boulder, we ride sideways on a cushion of river and are forced against its flank before being pulled into a black hole. The raft's bow doubles back on itself as we crash into a solid stopper of dark water that hits me squarely in the chest, pouring over the boat, filling it with its weight. As I catch my breath, we drop down the other side of the wave into a second hole that seems to suck at the raft and hold us easily; white-water waves pour in before we are released to the far side of the river, where a whirlpool spins us full-circle, finally spitting us free into the calm below the fall. Soaked and

wide-eyed, we break into yells of laughter that fill the green valley and drain our adrenalin.

Gliding down the Seti River is like opening a geological text book. At the water's edge, where the rocks are exposed and washed clean, the steeply-angled strata are clearly visible, rising as cliffs in the gorge-like sections of the valley. Sometimes these cliffs reveal the tortuous folding and phenomenal forces of tectonic collision, where the rock appears to have been bent and twisted as easily as our rubber raft was by the river.

Downstream the Seti joins the waters of the Trisuli Gandaki that now lends its name to the river. Late in the afternoon, in a sunless section of the valley, we begin to feel the chill, until thankfully we meander around a spur into golden light. Great shafts of sun fan down from a tree-covered ridge, spotlighting a sandy beach at the water's edge.

Camp is soon set and a fire starts crackling. The beach is quickly made to feel like home, as mugs are filled with steaming tea and we laze in the mellow evening sun. Two boys paddling a narrow dug-out canoe ferry-glide across the river to our camp and sell us bananas and spinach. The silver sand is warm and silky long after the sun has set, as we sit around the camp fire, reliving the day and sipping duty-free Laphroag.

Passing beneath the parabola of a narrow suspension bridge a small rapid leads below low cliffs topped by temples at the confluence of the Trisuli and the Kali Gandaki; this is the sacred site and place of pilgrimage known as Devaghat. Above the confluence on the cliffs there are temples and shrines, said to date from the third and fourth centuries. Whilst the others had lunch on a sandy beach I ran up to see 'Crazy Baba', a Sardhu living by the temples. An archetypal giggling guru of the 1960s, Baba got himself the prefix 'Crazy' for his acts of self-mutilation. Bit by bit over the years he has been chopping off parts of his arm as an act of faith.

When I last visited him he was beyond the elbow. Apart from that he seems as sane as the next man, and quite 'armless'!

Leaving the mountains far behind, the Mahabharat gave way to the gentler Siwaliks, like ripples spreading outwards from a stone dropped into a pool. Unlike ripples in water, the solid geology of the Siwalik Hills ends abruptly, sharply defined against the endless flatness of the silt and gravel plain that extends south into India and Mother Ganga. In fact, they run from the Indus to the Brahmaputra in an almost continuous belt and were referred to by the ancient Aryans as 'the edge of the roof of Shiva's Himalayan abode'.

Now there were more people and settlements, with fields coming to the water's edge. The river twisted and turned across a broad flood plain, undoubtedly submerged during the monsoon, where thin cattle and coat-hanger-hipped buffalo grazed the sparse grass. Kites and carrion circled in the hot sky and a group of women waded the river carrying heavy bundles of wood collected from the dried-out plain. On either side of the river stands of rosewood alternated with flat fields being turned by oxen dragging wooden ploughs. Clutches of long, low, thatched houses sought shade under sparse trees and huge orange-flowered kapoks. Large yellow pumpkins nestled in the thatch like giant eggs in a nest, their twisting vines spiralling up roof timbers. There was a sense of order and timelessness, and the pace of life was echoed in the now unhurried river.

Then the forest closed in again on either side of the river (now the Narayani), forming the western boundary of Chitwan, and we bobbled over a shallow riffle where two streams converged depositing their gravel. On a mid-stream sand-bank the long snouted form of a *gharhial* (fish-eating crocodile), basked in the sun, reminding us that we were in the Terai and entering Chitwan. Pairs of brightly-coloured Brahmani ducks bobbed like marker buoys in

Praying on the banks of the Kali Gandaki at Devaghat.

the current. The forest of Chitwan is an open tangle of sal oak and silk-cotton trees with little in the way of undergrowth. In open glades, tall, feathery grasses conceal a wealth of wildlife. Unlike the plains of the African Savannah, where the endless open prairies of short grass make for easy travel and game viewing, here movement is difficult and the wildlife elusive. Before we reached our final mooring our skilful coxswain manoeuvred our craft around unseen obstacles in the silky water so silently that a confused *chital*, a spotted deer, stood rigid on the bank paired with its perfect mirror image as we drifted by. Time after time the black shapes of 'crocodiles' turned out to be logodiles, much to the amusement of our Gurung crew.

A dug-out being paddled across the Trisuli Khola beyond the Siwalik Hills.

A camp for working elephants in Chitwan.

As with everything at Tiger Tops, the timing was immaculate. We were met on the river bank by Terai taxis, fine female elephants resplendent with *howdahs* and *mahoots*. Four to an elephant, we trampled our stately way, trunk to tail, to the lodge, an orderly oasis, and a place to be pampered and educated by wildlife experts and ornithologists. Given that most people spend only a few days in Chitwan, there can be no better place to relax and enjoy the experience. After the climbing expedition and life afloat, Tiger Tops came as a culture shock. The central lodge is definitely 'colonial revivalist', with dinner served by flawless stewards around a huge central fire. Propping up the bar afterwards, Dr Charles McDougal, the lodge's director and a world authority on the tiger, chatted about the preserve and spun yarns about big cats in Chitwan. I retired to my tree-top bedroom happy with my lot and looking forward to an elephant-top safari in the morning.

After breakfast I climbed aboard my elephant straight from the bedroom balcony! Knowing I was there to get photographs, the organizers had provided me with a personal 'jumbo' with an especially accommodating driver. Leaving the parade of elephants we twisted and turned, allowing me to get the angles I wanted. Despite its bulk, the elephant's movements were more delicate than can be imagined. Sure-footed, it paced down slippery inclines and waded streams, quietly parting the tall grass like an ice-breaker through a frozen sea. Tree-house high, I shared the branches of the forest with its many birds and monkeys. Following a narrow track through the sal and silk-cotton trees we surprised a small group of barking-deer, and were in turn surprised ourselves by the hair-raising scream of a peacock which was roosting in a nearby tree.

On the edge of a clearing where the tall grass had been burned off, a female rhino and young calf were grazing. More ancient-looking than their African brothers, their plate armour skin seems truly prehistoric, like the one-horned *Tricerotops*. Unafraid of the elephant (or simply myopic), they were hardly bothered by our presence but continued to browse on the fresh shoots and shrubs.

Ducking through a thicket of sal trees and twisted vines, small hornbills and brightly-coloured kingfishers flashed along the edge of a water course. Emerging from the wood into bright sunlight on the edge of a meadow of tall plumbed grass, my transport suddenly stopped. Her front legs were rigid, as if she was trying to brake on a steep incline, and a shock-wave of trembling, like a distant earth tremor, vibrated through her bulk. Then I saw it. Larger than I imagined, its colour brighter — a startling orange — and its markings more vivid. The moment, like the elephant's gait, froze. It was a brief encounter, just long enough to remember, to snatch a photograph, and then, as with the elephant, a shock-wave of excitement ran through my body. I had seen the Bengal tiger. In 1921 the Prince of Wales, later to become Edward VIII, hunted in Chitwan (as George V had done ten years earlier) with a party that numbered 300, and engaging over 400 elephants. It's sad to record that the kill included eighteen tigers, ten rhino, two leopards and a similar number of bear.

I wanted to visit a local village outside of the park and to meet some local Tharus, the original inhabitants of Chitwan and the Terai. A Land Rover drove me to the river where a dug-out canoe ferried me to the far bank. In the distance, beyond the Siwaliks and Mahabharat Lekh, the icy peaks of Himalchuli and Manaslu were floating ethereal above a shroud of mist.

I spent the day wandering a neat Tharu village set out along a dirt track through a landscape of fields yellow with mustard. So unlike the mountain farmers who struggle to cultivate the stony slopes, the Tharus seemed prosperous from the soil and its abundant water. Their origin is obscure. One suggestion is that they migrated from Thar in Sindh; others say that they are people of Rajput stock who fled to Nepal in the face of Muslim attack, and that the tattoos on the feet and hands of the women are offensive to Muslims, protecting them from rape.

Wherever you go in Nepal it is impossible not to feel like the Hamelin rat-catcher. I have this vision of harassed mothers all over Nepal giving a sigh of relief when a trekking party comes through, and telling their bored offspring to 'go outside and annoy the tourists'. Fortunately the children hadn't developed the habit of begging for *mitai* and *bon-bons*, as most on the popular trek routes do.

The Tharus are an attractive race. The men, small in stature, have muscular, stocky frames, and thus seem closer to mountain rather than Aryan types. They work in the fields dressed in shorts or a simple loin cloth (*kachhad*). The women, wearing cotton saris or a short blouse (*cholo*) and cotton wrap skirt, work on the verandahs winnowing rice in large, brightly-decorated, flat straw baskets. As well as the

Buffalo in a water-hole, doing what they like best.

hand tattoos, most wear a tight bracelet above their elbow. When I was there, others were smearing the wattle of their thatched houses with white river mud. Unlike so many homes in the hills, these were swept and orderly. Most of the houses were decorated with hand-painted murals that included fish shapes and finger decoration, and harvest corn-dollies decorated the eaves.

Finding a place where I could buy tea, I sat under the shade of a hay loft listening to the coo-cooing from a dovecote. I assume that the Tharus breed and eat the birds or at least the eggs, since most houses had some kind of cot. Finding me interested in everything Tharu, from basketwork to finger painting, a young man who had been mending a large wooden ox-cart led me into a nearby field where the crops had been trampled. It was easy to pinpoint the culprit. The ground was puddled by the three-toed imprint of the rhino. It's surprising that many more tiger haven't turned man-eater with the settlements so close to the park. However in many of the fields there are tall watch-towers manned when villagers are working on the land.

But the future of Chitwan and the Tharus must seem uncertain. For the park, the expansion of tourism might result in more lodges being built; Nepal can certainly do with the foreign funds. On the other hand, more people will undoubtedly disturb this serene habitat and perhaps its delicate balance as an ecosystem. For the Tharus, as for the wild animals, there is pressure on the land where they live. As Nepal's population grows, cultivation on marginal hill land increases to the point where saturation strips the land of its primary cover, leading to massive erosion as soil is washed to the rivers. In the Terai there is an abundance of flat, tillable land. Since malaria ceased to be a problem there has been a steady influx of hill-people that was heightened by a reclamation and resettlement programme. Harkur Gurung gives the population of the Terai in the 1950s as 40,000, and it had increased by 1961 to a reasonable 67,882. However, a decade later, as a result of resettlement, the population had increased to 193,644. Almost two decades of the growth continues with the expansion of towns like Narayanghat. I am hopeful. Since that first visit I have returned many times to 'shoot' the elusive tiger and glimpse the Gangetic dolphin. The park has more lodges now, some not run by naturalists or sympathetic directors, and there are more tourists, but the quiet forest and tall grass have absorbed them all so far . . .

At the end of my few days in the Terai I had drunk my 'beaker-full of the warm south' and had my moments of 'sunburnt mirth'; now it was time to turn again to the north and seek new paths into Jugal.

RIVER RUNNING:

Several commercial companies have now been established that organize and outfit rafting trips on rivers in Nepal, of which the Sun Khosi is amongst the most sustained. The Seti and Trisuli are more moderate and amongst the most popular. Himalayan River Exploration, the first such company in Nepal, remains at the forefront.

GAME VIEWING AND ELEPHANT SAFARIS:

These are becoming increasingly popular within Royal Chitwan. Tiger Tops remains the most exclusive and the most expensive, with outstanding facilities and unequalled quality. They also run a Tented Camp and a Tharu Village long house. They have highly-trained naturalists and maintain a low impact on

the environment and its animals. Gaida Jungle Camp and Hotel Elephant Camp also provide game viewing and elephant safaris.

Safaris can be booked direct through agents in Kathmandu. Most Adventure Travel agents offering treks to Nepal also offer an extension to Chitwan. *See* Useful Addresses.

LOGISTICS:

There are regular flights to Meghauli from Kathmandu. A new road has also been built from Mugling through Narayangarh to Meghauli, taking in Kasara, the Park Headquarters. A road also connects with Saura from Narayangarh via Tadi Bazar, where there are lodges. Visitors entering the park independently pay a fee which also includes the services of a guide.

SEASON:

The post-monsoon months and especially the spring are ideal for wildlife viewing. The Terai is also very hot in April and May.

(Left) Tharu girls on the bank of the Narayani River at the end of a long day of harvesting.

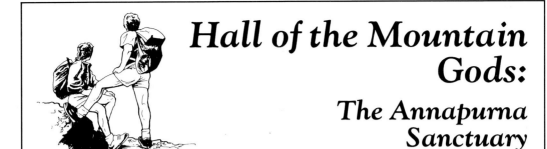

Hall of the Mountain Gods:

The Annapurna Sanctuary

Just go on and on ... Do you see the mountain ranges there, far away? One behind another. They rise up. They tower. That is my deep, unending inexhaustible Kingdom.

Henrik Ibsen
The Master Builder

From the sub-tropical lakeside of Phewi Tal on the outskirts of Pokhara, 200 bumpy km (135 miles) by road from Kathmandu, you can marvel at the mirrored image of one of the most stunning mountain panoramas in the Himalaya. Isolated between two great rivers, the Kali Gandaki and the Marsyangdi Khola, soars the Annapurna Himal, a forty-mile bastion of massive mountains, twelve of which rise above 7,000m (22,960ft). Despite the early exploration and perambulation of its lateral and northern flanks, the southern boundary remained a blank on the mountaineer's map. Quite understandably so, since this is a complex area of deep river gorges, including those of the Modi, Seti and Mardi Khola, whose genesis is in the steep glaciers to the north through which there is no obvious passage. Separating these rivers are precipitous and densely-wooded ridges, spreading from the Himal like the fingers of an outstretched hand. Despite the fact that the area is heavily populated, early explorers naturally followed the major trans-Himalayan routeways, trailing the great rivers rather than

the cul-de-sac paths of their subordinate streams.

However, in the cornucopia of mountains seen from Pokhara is a peak whose form alone isolates it from the mass. Often referred to as the 'Himalayan Matterhorn', the distincitve form of Machhapuchhare's twin summits resembles a fish's tail — this, for the local Hindus, is the embodiment of Shiva. Like most of the Himalaya, the 'Abode of Snow' is also the abode of the gods and in their local name can be found the incarnation of a deity. The sacred summit of the 'Fish Tail Peak' is no exception.

In 1956 Major J.O.M. 'Jimmy' Roberts MC, on one of his many exploits in the Nepal Himal, followed the course of the Modi Khola northwards during a reconnaissance of Machhapuchhare. From the Gurung village of Chomrong he continued between the portals of Hiunchuli and the 'Fish Tail', into the bamboo forests swathing the narrow Modi Gorge. Following hunters' tracks he noted a large undercut boulder, used by the locals as a bivouac, its roof blackened by countless fires. This spot, known as 'Hinko Cave', marked the entrance to a mountain amphitheatre fringed by peaks and filled by glaciers from which the Modi Khola sprang. When Roberts passed the small shrine at Panchenin Barha, at the very gateway to the hidden cwm, he noted that there was a local taboo forbidding women, men of menial caste, pork, chicken and eggs from going further

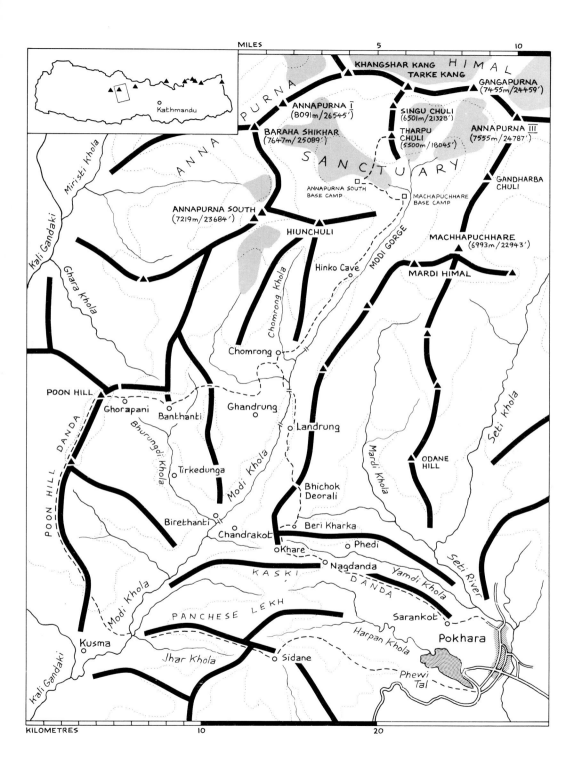

Kathmandu

KHANGSHAR KANG   HIMAL
TARKE KANG
ANNA   PURNA
GANGAPURNA
(7455m/24459′)
ANNAPURNA I
(8091m/26545′)
SINGU CHULI
(6501m/21328′)
ANNAPURNA III
(7555m/24787′)
BARAHA SHIKHAR
(7647m/25089′)
THARPU
CHULI
(5500m/18045′)
ANNA
SANCTUARY
GANDHARBA
CHULI
Miristi Khola
Kali Gandaki
ANNAPURNA SOUTH
BASE CAMP
MACHAPUCHHARE
BASE CAMP
ANNAPURNA SOUTH
(7219m/23684′)
HIUNCHULI
MACHHAPUCHHARE
(6993m/22943′)
Ghara Khola
Chomrong Khola
Hinko Cave
MODI GORGE
MARDI HIMAL
Chomrong
POON HILL
Ghorapani
Banthanti
Ghandrung
Landrung
Seti Khola
POON HILL DANDA
Bhurungdi Khola
Tirkedunga
Modi Khola
Mardi Khola
ODANE
HILL
Bhichok
Deorali
Birethanti
Chandrakot
Beri Kharka
Khare
Phedi
KASKI
Nagdanda
Yamdi Khola
DANDA
Seti River
Modi Khola
PANCHESE LEKH
Sarankot
Harpan Khola
Pokhara
Kusma
Jhar Khola
Sidane
Phewi
Tal
Kali Gandaki

and entering this sacred basin; he described it appropriately as the 'Annapurna Sanctuary'.

Today 'The Sanctuary' is a popular destination for hardier trekkers, and although it's often linked with the circuit of Annapurna, it provides in its own right an enjoyable and relatively short trek into the very heart of a mountain wilderness, and the foot of the world's thirteenth-highest peak.

As well as being a perfect trekking destination there is within The Sanctuary a plexus of smaller listed trekking peaks; not simply hill walkers' mountains, but smaller Himalayan summits, more on an Alpine scale, that can be climbed with little more red tape and expense than that required in getting a Trekking Peak Permit. However, a journey into The Sanctuary, whether to climb or not, will always be a memorable experience.

We left Kathmandu in the hour before dawn to drive westwards to Pokhara. Forgoing the dubious pleasure of the public bus, we had opted for the comfort of a private one. With a guarantee from the hire company that it would be a Mercedes, only the logo on the bonnet was an indication that it was, or at least had that pedigree. Undoubtedly it must have arrived with the first wave of hippies in the sixties and, having fought its way over the Khyber, had since been Nepali-ized! The seats, as in the tourist section of most Jumbos, had been pushed too close together. Although such seats might be utter luxury to tiny Asians, who would have no trouble sitting cross-legged in a cardboard shoe-box, the average gaunt European finds sitting straight-backed with his knees jammed under his chin, wedged against the back of the seat in front, a moving hell. Comfort, however, is a relative issue and the lack of it can be endured — driving Nepali style is another matter. Only a multitude of Ganesh postcards, and the whole of the Hindu and Buddhist pantheon stuck to the inside of the screen,

convinced me that we had any chance of covering safely the convoluted washboard that serves as the road to Pokhara.

Beyond the dirty windows and diesel fumes of the interior was the beautiful contrast of a new day. As we climbed out of a mist-filled Kathmandu Valley, the morning sun on the distant summits made them seem like flickering gas flames, glowing pink and warm above purple shadow. The road westwards parallels the peaks, providing a panorama that stretches from Langtang to the Annapurnas, doubly compensating for the adventure of the ride. Helter-skelter down tight switchbacks, and at times above deep river drops, along an unmetalled road prone to landslides and rockfall, we ploughed on. Blasting westwards in the face of everything, including the desperate haste of grossly overloaded oncoming buses, we watched, perplexed by the paradox of it all.

Beyond the bus, village life in Nepal has no apparent haste. With first light cocks crow and dogs bark — heralds to the new day. Women wrapped in thin cotton shawls emerge from dark doorways carrying small sickles and silent babies, to walk barefoot into wet-fields of rice for a day of bent-backed labour. Older ragged children defecate unselfconsciously by the roadside or drive animals from their byres to nearby grazing, taking time to play and talk. Men and women huddle sociably together over baskets heavy with giant white radishes, tethered chickens and gunni-sacs of grain to barter one against the other. All this is glimpsed enviably from the pandemonium of the bus, and it's only during the reasoned pace on trek that we can become part of it.

By the time we arrived in Pokhara, after hours spent negotiating a landslide where a flooding stream had washed away the road, it was too late to press on up the Kaski Danda. Instead we camped by the lakeside on its north shore, where, despite the lodges, shops, cafes and campsites, there is a general air of tranquillity.

The mirrored image of the Annapurna Himal in Phewi Tal, a forty-mile bastion of massive mountains between the Kali Gandaki and the Marsyangdi Khola.

After swimming I wandered along the road into town, stopping for 'tea and stickies' at a Vienna-style coffee house (run appropriately by 'flower-power' Germans), before going to call on Jimmy Roberts.

Jimmy first visited Pokhara in 1950 after the Tilman-led expedition into Manang. Believing then, as now, that 'there is no other mountain view in the world to equal Machhapuchhare and Annapurna, hanging there in the sky above the green Pokhara plain', he has lived there much of the time since. After serving as Military Attaché at the British Embassy in Kathmandu, he went on to organize the first commercial treks in Nepal. Still intimately involved with Mountain Travel, the company he founded in 1964, he now has a pheasant farm in Pokhara, run in co-operation with the World Pheasant Association, with all manner of exotic and endangered birds which are used to restock the wild. A shy and humorous man, he has an unequalled knowledge of Nepal and its mountains, based on first-hand experience and exploration.

Before bed tea was being served, and as the porters hired by our Sirdar assembled around camp, I left for the opposite bank. Having organised a canoe to take me to the southern shore, I wanted to stare at Jimmy's incomparable view enhanced by sunrise and its equally stunning image in the deep green waters of the lake. By the time I had returned the usual breakfast of tea and biscuits and a bowl of porridge was being devoured, whilst the first of the black kites that glide over and dive the lake was eyeing my portion from on high.

Following a line of lean-legged porters, we traipsed through the streets of Pokhara, passing a bustling, straggling town of open-fronted brick houses and stores to Mahendra Pul, from where overloaded jeeps ply up the Yamdi Khola Valley to Phedi. Leaving the dusty road behind, we climbed steeply up the ridge separating the valley from the lake. A hot and tiring climb of

900 metres, it gains the crest of the Kaski Danda near the old fort of Sarankot (1,583m/5,200ft). Once gained, the ridge offers superb hiking, with magnificent glimpses of Machhapuchhare and the eastern Annapurnas.

Pokhara is lower than Kathmandu and the vegetation and temperature are definitely sub-tropical. Walking in the full glare of the sun can be wilting for the first few days, and this is only partially relieved by whatever breeze the ridge-walk affords. Now, as on treks past, we made good use of the large, black umbrellas bought for a few rupees in the bazaar. Still finding my walking feet, I leap-frogged group members cooling off inside t-shops sipping soft drinks.

It was good to be on the open, wide trail passing through highly cultivated yet very attractive farmland, studded with charming hipped-thatch Chettri houses and stands of vivid, green-leafed bamboo. At Sanri Pokhari I stopped to photograph a small shrine near the reservoir and was joined by a multitude of uniformed schoolchildren who practised well-mouthed English phrases on me to the delight and laughter of their peers. Shortly after the tea shop at Kashikot Deorali, the path descended towards Naudanda.

This is a busy little town set in a notch in the ridge at the junction of many paths, including the one from Phedi, which is the small gaggle of houses at the foot of the steep slope below. Having reported at the police post for a permit check, we continued through the town with its many lodges and stalls, past the stud farm, taking the right-branching trail up the stone steps towards Khare. Situated on a ridge at the head of the Yamdi Khola, the main trail descends the far side to Chandrakot and the Modi Khola. Opting for a less-travelled route, we turned right at Prem Lodge but not before we had bought a glass of sweet, boiled buffalo-milk tea. Traversing the head of the Yamdi Valley, past a well constructed *chautarra*, we entered a cool, damp forest where verdant moss-covered branches supported epiphitic orchids. This was in sharp contrast to the well-trekked track and open farmland we had left behind.

We camped that night on the ridge on the far side of the Yamdi Valley at a place called Beri Kharka (2,050m/6,726ft). It was a wonderful spot — flat, and near to some large rhododendron trees on top of a rocky bluff, below which was a comfortable cave used by porters. But best of all was the view. Seen through a gap in the branches, Annapurna South and Hiunchuli dominated the scene north-westwards, providing a perfect setting. Not far from here, after the traverse of a densely-wooded hillside, was the settlement of Tanchok Potana, with its gaggle of lodges and t-shops. Since my first visit five years earlier it had obviously been a victim of the tourist boom.

An hour or so further on, after passing ruined buildings, the route follows a ridge-top path through glorious stands of rhododendrons to gain the notch at Bhichok Deorali (2,113m/6,932ft), where an enterprising Gurung has built a tiny t-shop.

Ahead lay the valley of the Modi Khola. Descending the west side of the small *deorali* (col), the path descended steeply in places through damp forest where slippery roots made the path difficult after recent rain. Many of our porters removed their rubber thongs to get a surer footing with their almost prehensile toes. The action of their carefully-planted feet searching out the best places to step was a mockery of the noisy footfalls of the trekkers lurching and sliding down the same slope.

Several small lodges had sprung up since I was here last, offering extensive menus. Beware the Nepali *bhatti* at midday, especially if you intend to cover a good distance in the afternoon. Not because the food is heavy in the stomach, but rather because of the time it invariably takes to make and cook a complicated individual order. A serving of *momos* say, prepared and cooked fresh, can take an hour, or longer (far longer) in

A hipped thatch house typical of the Gurung village of Landrung in the Modi Khola.
Beyond are Annapurna South and Hiunchuli above the Chomrong Khola.

a crowded lodge, where your order may wait whilst easier dishes are cooked. It is far better to stick to simple *dhalbhaat* or omelette and chapatti, and not have to stay the night!

Staying high above the east bank of the Modi Khola, the path looks out over extensively terraced farmland. It passes through neat Gurung homes, many of them with circular red ochre walls and thatched roofs. Beyond the Tolka Lodge we were met by a village representative carrying a book signed by trekkers who had made a donation to the Shri Lower Secondary School. Faced with such enterprise I also obliged, noting that if it was a scam my contribution was unlikely to rocket him into the super-tax bracket.

In places the path traversed under steep vegetated cliffs adorned with trailing orchids. Shortly afterwards, above a totally deforested hillside, we crossed a stream with bathing pools and entered Landrung (5,400ft), a tidy Gurung village strung out along the hillside path. On

the far side of the deep Modi Valley, a little higher than Landrung, is the larger Gurung village of Ghandrung.

Until recently it was necessary to descend to the river and cross a suspension bridge and climb to Ghandrung if your destination was Chomrong and The Sanctuary. However, this is no longer the case now that a new bridge has been built further upstream.

Close to the new bridge we found a delightful clearing near the river. Rather than push on, we decided to camp and slumped against large water-worn boulders in a grassy meadow to await the arrival of the loads. From a vantage point on top of a rock I saw Andy, a member of my group and a gentle giant who always found time to sketch or paint at every stop no matter how brief, surrounded by a sea of gently-waving black and green grass. In amused horror I realised that the black blades were the outstretched, searching suckers of leeches, and that our damp meadow was their ideal breeding ground. With

A Gurung woman winnowing grain.

a reaction reminiscent of a scalded cartoon cat, he vacated the grass and joined me on the leech-free rock to discover that he was both bleeding and being sucked dry by what looked now like bloated slugs! Leeches are amazing creatures — they wait on branches or in damp grass, living in hope of a passing meal from man or beast. If they get lucky, they attach themselves unnoticed and invariably depart unseen, leaving a bleeding, punctured circle. Getting undressed one night I found nine of the little bleeders, like babes at the breast, firmly attached and sucking away contentedly.

Once over the river the path climbs steeply to Chamru, an area that illustrates well the increasing demand on marginal land in Nepal. Here a few hard-working Gurung families have literally carved a living from the steeply wooded

slopes. Elsewhere along this section of the trail, in fact all the way to Chomrong, small lodges wait for trekkers. We stopped at the Tinimini Lodge before we made the steep climb up the crest of the Gimnu Danda. It was hot in the full glare of the sun, and we stopped frequently to cool off and take in the view of Gangapurna at the head of the Sanctuary.

At Taulu we met the path from Ghandrung and a few other trekkers. The word was out that there was a lot of snow in the Sanctuary and the lodges beyond Hinko were closed, so those that didn't have tents and equipment to look after themselves were put off. It was interesting to see the effect that the recently-initiated Annapurna Conservation Area Project was having. Several of the lodges had installed more efficient cooking fires and the larger ones had solar panels for heating water. Hopefully the project will help both to preserve the environment and allow locals some prosperity from tourism.

Chomrong is a thriving Gurung village set high above the Chomrong Khola, opposite the impressive south wall of Annapurna South and Hiunchuli (inappropriately called a trekking peak). This is the last major settlement before the Sanctuary and has a booming tourist business. Our trekking permits were again checked, and the man in the ACAP office was able to sell us some paraffin for the primus stoves we had been using on our journey to the Sanctuary.

Ahead the character of the trek changed totally. Having climbed out of the rift of the Chomrong Khola, we traversed high above the Modi River on its precipitous western bank into the impressive gorge between Machhapuchhare and Hiunchuli that provides the 'gateway' to the Annapurna Sanctuary.

We made our way through a forest of dense bamboo, overhung by beetling cliffs made more dramatic by swirling cloud. The path was very narrow and the dripping bamboo and wet tree roots were like black ice underfoot. In several places a slip would have been difficult to stop, with the river below a long way down and the boulders nasty to land on.

In a landscape reminiscent of a Japanese watercolour, small lodges emerged from the misty bamboo, a welcome respite on this cold, damp day. On the left were waterfalls cascading in a silky curtain down the lower rock-walls of Hiunchuli. After traversing close to the river the trail followed tunnels through the bamboo until finally it climbed steeply to the huge overhanging boulder of Hinko Cave. A small t-shop had been built under the smoke-blackened eaves, and it was here that we waited to assemble our whole party before going on to camp before an unseen danger.

Ahead the vegetation thins and the route goes close to the river, presenting no problem. However, it is threatened by a hidden glacier on Hiunchuli. A huge avalanche cone covered the trail, a deadly manifestation of the menace from above. Aware that several trekkers had been killed on this section, and wary of the danger posed by recent heavy rain and snow, I wanted to get my group safely over this part.

Leaving early in the morning, hopefully before the sun had warmed the icefall above, we crossed the avalanche debris rapidly, alert for the sound and sight of danger. Still in deep shadow we crossed the last of several cones before the t-shop at Baga, where we waited for the tailenders to catch up. As I counted the last man in a thunderous roar rebounded from the cliffs of the canyon, as a heavy mass of wet snow, ice blocks and rock shot over the cliff in the line of a waterfall, thudding on to the cone we had just crossed, before damming the river and piling up the moraine on the far side. We had passed through the 'gate' and had entered the 'Sanctuary of the Gods.'

The earlier snow was now covering the trail as we hiked along a moraine crest to the site of Machhapuchhare Base Camp (3,658m/ 12,000ft), where beneath several metres of snow

From the moraines below Tharpu Chuli the North West Face of Machhapuchhare (6,993m/22,943ft) stands as a portal to the Annapurna Sanctuary.

a recently-built trekkers lodge was buried. Glaringly beautiful under a duvet of fresh snow, the skyline was a circle of peaks barely breached by the Modi Gorge.

Westwards from the summit of Hiunchuli an icy ridge connects it to Annapurna South (7,219m/23,684ft), before sweeping on in a crenelated crest northwards to Baraha Shikhar (7,647m/25,089ft) and the sacred summit of Annapurna 1 (8,091m/26,545ft), Shiva's consort. The circle then turns eastwards through several summits, including Glacier Dome, to the deity of Gangapurna (7,455m/24,459ft), before it closes southwards to Annapurna 3 (7,555m/ 24,787ft) and Annapurna 5 (7,525m/24,688ft). It ends finally in the symbol of Shiva himself — Machhapuchhare.

We turned north-west following an ablation valley filled with deep soft snow, aiming for the sight of Annapurna South Base Camp (not to be confused with the original Annapurna Base Camp which is on the other side of the mountain). Escaping from the drudgery of the snow, I gained the crest of the lateral moraine of the South Annapurna Glacier, a narrow crest with a precipitous drop to the north. From the crest of the moraine the form of the Sanctuary is clearer and it becomes obvious that from the backwall of ice, Glacier Dome throws southwards a narrow ridge that literally divides the circle in two. On this divide rise two distinct summits separating the South and West Annapurna Glaciers. The most distant of these, Singu Chuli (6,501m/21,328ft), presents 'a beautiful shape buttressed by pencil-shadowy ridges of snow and ice', which in turn connects with Tharpu Chuli (5,500m/18,045ft) just across the glacier. Both of these mountains are official trekking peaks.

We arrived at Base Camp with not a building in sight; in fact there are several stone huts with bamboo thatch roofs that serve as simple lodges, but these were under several metres of snow. Locating a hut, we dug a vertical tunnel into the snow, and climbed through the roof to a perfectly dry interior. Having found the real door it was simply a matter of burrowing an entrance at a more conventional angle. Whilst the Sherpas set to with a vengeance, we pitched our tents in the glaring afternoon sun.

We spent a couple of days exploring what we could of this wonderful sanctuary. Conditions wouldn't allow an ascent of Tharpu Chuli this time so we cut short our stay and returned to Chomrong. My feelings about failing to do a climb echoed the words of Sir Martin Conway writing about the Karakoram in 1891:

Romance almost became a reality. The gods were very near at hand. We touched as it were the skirts of their garments. Yet even at the culminating moments of these strenuous dream-days there still lingered the sense of incompleteness, of something lacking. The secret was almost disclosed, but never quite, the veil never entirely withdrawn.

But these feelings were soon dispersed when I decided that, rather than returning down the valley by way of Ghandrung to Pokhara, we would skirt westwards beneath the massive rampart of Annapurna South to Banthanti and on to Ghorapani.

Ghorapani marks a notch in the watershed between the Bhurungdi Khola, a tributary of the Modi and Ghar Khola, a tributary of the Kali Gandaki, which in turn absorbs the Modi Khola near Kusma. The hike to Ghorapani, a rapidly-expanding settlement, is thoroughly worthwhile. It climbs and falls through rich forests of rhododendrons and magnolia that perfectly frame the stunning mountain skyline.

But it is above Ghorapani on Poon Hill that is regarded as the viewpoint of viewpoints. A simple hike a few hundred metres above the lodges, it can be reached almost without effort at dawn and sunset, when it provides an amazing view of the Dhaulagiri Himal seen across the Kali Gandaki gorge, whilst on the far side of the river the Annapurna and Nilgiri ranges make this the deepest river valley in the world.

I had brought the group to Poon Hill not simply to marvel at the view, but to follow a line I had long wanted to take on the return leg to Pokhara. Poon Hill in fact is simply the northern promontory of a ridge extending southwards towards Kusma, dividing the Modi and Kali Gandaki rivers. By following this high untrekked ridge southwards, I could connect with the Panchase Lekh and so return to the western end of Phewi Tal and Pokhara.

And so it was that, leaving Poon Hill soon after dawn, we tramped southwards, following at first a narrow trail along the ridge crest between massive stands of rhododendrons past several kharka, quickly leaving behind any trace of other trekkers. Exaggerated though it may seem, further south on the ridge of Poon Hill the panorama is even more extensive, with the Churen Himal and Himalchuli included in an even finer view. Difficult to follow, the faint path criss-crosses the ridge before descending into a hushed valley with a clear fresh stream, obviously a high kharka — perhaps for the people of Ulleri?

In all we trekked for two glorious days along this high pristine crest before meeting a well-made track, a high-level route between Beni and Kusma, that had several ancient stone rest houses. These were perhaps former barracks for the Ghurka armies that swarmed from the hills, following Prithvinarayan Shah in the eighteenth century, or were they the rest houses of Thakali merchants or the Malla rulers of Parbat in the seventeenth century?

After descending the southern end of the ridge through terraced hillsides we crossed a suspension bridge over the Modi Khola near Chuwa and camped on the far side, washing off the dust of several days' march by swimming in the Jhar Khola. We spent two more days hiking a circuitous route along the Panchase Lekh, where the heat was intense, despite the fact that the ridge line climbed to over 2,440m (8,000ft). At the Panchase Bhanjyang there was a small t-shop run by a smiling old woman, who was overwhelmed by the upsurge in business we brought. Sitting bemused and gratified at our apparently unquenchable demand for hot sweet *chai*, she ranted on, asking questions and laughing at our ridiculous answers, trying to tempt us to a stronger brew of *chang*. Reluctant to leave this oasis, we continued descending through lush rhododendrons and michelia forest that in turn gave way to terraced farmland and scattered settlements.

An endless descent down an interminable stone stairway and then through dusty terraced farmland towards Sidane at last brought us to a river and a place to swim. This densely-peopled

and intensely-farmed area was a total contrast to the untracked forested heights of the Poon Hill Danda, but the fact that the two were so different made the expedition all the more interesting. They did share one common factor though — throughout the hike from Poon Hill we met no other trekkers, and found not a single lodge beyond the odd traditional *bhatti* until we arrived back in Pokhara.

From a camp by the Harpan Khola, we woke early to a mist-filled dawn. Cattle egrets and larger heron were standing stiff-legged on grassy strands and in reed beds of isolated pools along the water's edge. The sunrise, when it came, was a slow, cool affair, like a slice of orange floating in a bowl of cream. It was in keeping with our mood, I suppose, now we were coming to the

A Gurung woman nurses her child on the trek to Ghorapani.

end of our journey, trudging the last few miles along the open gravel flats of the diminished river's bed to the western end of the lake. Above us to the north, emerging through the clearing mist, we could see the Kaski Danda and Sarankot — we had almost gone full circle. Now all that was left to be done was to pile into a canoe and paddle the last miles to Pokhara.

ITINERARY:

DAY 1: KATHMANDU TO POKHARA

Flying from Kathmandu is undoubtedly the easiest way. Can be reached by private and public bus in the day. A bumpy but enjoyable ride after which it is best to camp near the roadhead or by the lakeside.

DAYS 2 – 3: POKHARA TO BERI KHARKA

A steep climb to gain the Kaski Danda and Sarankot. Fine views and open walking along ridge. Numerous small settlements. Continue through Naudanda where there is a checkpost and plenty of traders. This can be reached by taking the road to Phedi and climbing from there, saving a day. Continue to Khare. Climb northwards around head of Yamdi Khola to gain ridge near Beri Kharka. Lodges at Bhichok or very good camping.

DAYS 3 – 4: BERI KHARKA TO CHOMRONG

Cross wooded ridge and enter Modi Valley. Continue past Landrung and numerous Gurung settlements. Stay on east flank of valley and continue to New Bridge. Good camping and lodges. Climb west bank of valley and eventually reach large village of Chomrong. ACAP office and checkpoint. Some kerosene supplies.

DAYS 5 – 7: CHOMRONG TO ANNAPURNA SOUTH BASE CAMP

Cross Chomrong Valley and continue above Modi Gorge through dense bamboo forest.

Numerous small settlements and lodges (some seasonal), check in Chomrong. Continue past Hinko to Baga then more steeply up moraines to lodge near Machhapuchhare Base Camp. Follow ablation valley or moraines on south bank of Annapurna South Glacier to lodges at Annapurna South Base Camp. This is a quick approach route with little acclimatization.

This approach provides the route to three listed trekking peaks: Hiunchuli, Tharpu Chuli and Singu Chuli. Details of these can be found in *Trekking Peaks of Nepal*, Bill O'Connor, (Crowood Press, 1989).

DAYS 8 – 10: BASE CAMP TO GHORAPANI

Return down Modi Gorge to Chomrong then continue to Banthanti and Ghorapani. Delightful walking through dense forest of magnolia and rhododendrons followed by glorious ridge-walking and fine views.

DAYS 11 – 12: GHORAPANI TO KUSMA

Follow the Poon Hill ridge southwards. Glorious wooded ridge; top tramping with extensive views. Meet path between Beni and Kusma. Continue to suspension bridge over Modi, camping near Chuwa.

DAYS 13 – 14: KUSMA TO POKHARA

Gain the Panchase Lekh and follow it through woods and pastures to Sidane. Hot walking, glorious flowers and birdlife, long descents. Camp near Harpan Khola. Follow valley to western end of Phewi Tal. Boat back to Pokhara or walk along north side of the lake.

Boy on a bamboo swing — a common sight during the Divali festival.

DIFFICULTY:

A straightforward trek with no great altitude, several long ascents and descents. There is some avalanche danger between Hinko and Machhapuchhare Base Camp. The final part along Pool Hill Danda is indistinct and without lodges.

LOGISTICS:

Access to Pokhara is straightforward, either from Kathmandu or direct by road from India. Trek permits can be obtained in Pokhara or Kathmandu. Paraffin has to be used inside the Annapurna Conservation Area by independent trekkers. There are lodges throughout the trek, except on the section from Poon Hill. Canoe transport is always available at the western end of Phewi Tal.

MAPS:

The available maps of the Annapurna Sanctuary area are poor for mountaineering use but adequate for trekking. It is very difficult to lose your way if you wish to keep to the main routes. Mandala or Yeti Productions dyeline maps, Pokhara to Jomosom Manang 1;125,000 sheet, cover the area.

EQUIPMENT:

Only normal trekking equipment is required for those wishing to go to Base Camp. Since there are no lodges on the Poon Hill ridge, independent trekkers will need to carry bivouac equipment or a small tent and some cooking gear. Beyond Kusma simple food can be had in small local *bhattis*.

Forbidden Kingdom:
Rolwaling Reopened/
Dhaulagiri/Dolpo

. . . What does the mountain care?
Ah, but a man's reach should exceed his grasp,
Or what's a heaven for?

Robert Browning
Andrea del Sarto

A trek in Nepal is like walking through the Garden of Eden — everything seems perfect. The weather can be great, the views glorious, the campsites idyllic and the Sherpa crew absolute saints, and even the food is better than expected. Suddenly you crest a ridge and look

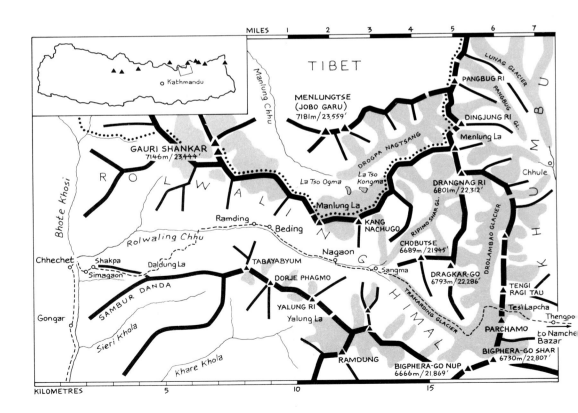

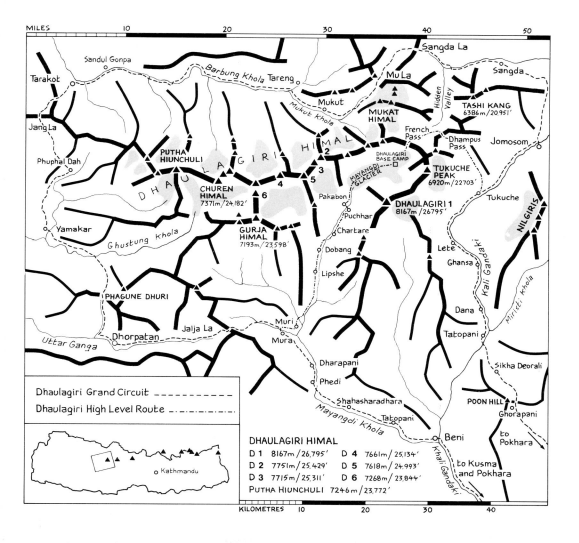

MILES · 10 · 20 · 30 · 40 · 50

Sandul Gonpa
Tarakot
Jang La
Phuphal Dah
Yamakar

Barbung Khola · Tareng
Mukut
Mukut Khola

Sangda La
Mu La
Sangda
MUKAT HIMAL
French Pass
Hidden Valley
TASHI KANG
6386m/20.951'
Dhampus Pass
Jomosom

PUTHA HIUNCHULI
DHAULAGIRI HIMAL
2
3
4 5
CHUREN HIMAL
737lm/24.182'
6
GURJA HIMAL
7193m/23.598'

Ghustung Khola

DHAULAGIRI BASE CAMP
MAYANGDI GLACIER
Pakaboni
Puchhar
Chartare
Dobang
Lipshe

TUKUCHE PEAK
6920m/22703'
DHAULAGIRI 1
8167m/26795'
Tukuche
Lete
Ghansa

NILGIRIS

Kali Gandaki
Miristi Khola

PHAGUNE DHURI
Dhorpatan
Jalja La
Muri
Mura
Dharapani
Phedi

Uttar Ganga

Dana
Tatopani
Sikha Deorali

Shahasharadhara
Mayangdi Khola
Tatopani
Beni

POON HILL
Ghorapani
to Pokhara
to Kusma and Pokhara

Khali Gandaki

Dhaulagiri Grand Circuit – – – – – –
Dhaulagiri High Level Route – · – · – · –

o Kathmandu

DHAULAGIRI HIMAL

D 1	8167m/26,795'	D 4	766lm/25,134'
D 2	775lm/25,429'	D 5	7618m/24,993'
D 3	7715m/25,311'	D 6	7268m/23,844'
PUTHA HIUNCHULI	7246m/23,772'		

KILOMETRES · 10 · 20 · 30 · 40

into a distant landscape — a deep river valley leading the eye longingly towards a line of snowy peaks — and you realize that they, like the apples in Eden, are forbidden fruit.

There is a lot of fruit available in the garden of Nepal, but still it's difficult not to be tempted by the apples. It would be so easy to turn north at Kagbeni for instance, after descending from the Thorong La, and venture into Mustang, the once self-governing enclave of Tibetan culture with its *dzongs* and *gompas* built of dried mud

blocks. I dream of wandering the trade routes through a landscape of glacial moraines sculptured by the elements into towers, like colossal termite mounds. But Mustang and its capital, Lo Monthang, remain out of reach.

On the Expedition Route to Everest the glimpses northwards are of Rolwaling Himal, an alluring temptress to the adventurous trekker that for much of the last decade was closed, but thankfully has now been reopened. This high valley extends eastwards as a tributary of the

Bhote Khosi to the Omai Tsho and Tsho Rolpo lake at the snout of the Trakarding Glacier, which in turn leads to the Tesi Laptsa at the foot of Tengi-Ragi Tau (6,943m/22,779ft) and the junction with the Khumbu. Its alluring skyline extends from the twinned summits of Gauri Shankar (7,146m/23,440ft), through the formidable, ice-hung wedge of Menlungtse (7,181m/23,560ft), whose lower summit was recently climbed by a British expedition led by Chris Bonington. Towards the eastern end of the range the icy curtain of Chobutse leads to Bigphero-Go Shar (6,730m/22,080ft), Numbur (6,955m/22,817ft), and Karyolung (6,511m/21,360ft) on the border of the Lumding Himal.

It was to the Rolwaling in search of the route to Everest that Tilman's party had hoped to go in 1949. In fact, the first Western exploration had to wait until Eric Shipton's Everest Reconnaissance of 1951. During this expedition Shipton with Mike Ward, followed later by Bill Murray and Tom Bourdillon, crossed the Menlung La north of Pangbug Ri (6,716m/22,034ft), descending eventually down the Ripimo Glacier to Beding in the Rolwaling

Valley. It was on this sortie that Shipton photographed the now famous Yeti prints. In the meantime the other members of the expedition, consisting of Hillary, Riddiford and Dutt, crossed the Tesi Lapcha, rejoining them at Beding before returning to Kathmandu. After this expedition Shipton wrote enthusiastically to *The Times*.

This form of mountaineering, the exploration of unknown peaks, glaciers and valleys, the finding and crossing of new passes to connect one area with another, is the most fascinating occupation I know. The variety of experience, the constantly changing scene, the gradual unfolding of the geography of the range are deeply satisfying, for they yield a very real understanding, almost a sense of personal possession, of the country explored.

A year later in 1952, whilst the Swiss were on Everest, a Cho Oyu Expedition, again under the leadership of Shipton, returned to Rolwaling and Tesi Lapcha where he, Alf Gregory and Charles Evans came close to climbing Pacharmo (6,273m/20,581ft). They would have succeeded,

Watching the sunrise from Poon Hill — 'fingers of light grasp the sky from behind the standing stone of Machhapuchhare'.

The moon setting behind Tagi Ragi Tau at the eastern end of the Rolwaling, rising between Tesi Lapcha to the south and the Menlung La.

had they not been persuaded by Shipton that it was more sporting to try it without crampons!

Bill Murray also returned to Rolwaling, in 1952, leading a group of Scottish mountaineers that completed three first ascents.

But the expedition that epitomizes everything that is best about the free-ranging lightweight style was the Merseyside Himalayan Expedition of 1955, under the leadership of Alf Gregory. During the course of the expedition this four-man team climbed nineteen summits, many of them obviously first ascents. Their explorations were extensive, taking them south of the Rolwaling Valley, on peaks such as Ramdung and Panayo Tippa (6,696m/21,968ft). It was to the north of the valley, however, that their exploration was most extensive, especially into the Menlung Basin as far north as Kangkuru (6,263m/20,550ft), a peak north of the Menlung La. Their circumambulation of the Chobutse group, which included ascents of Dragkar-Go and a 20,000 footer just south of Dragnag Ri, must have been a splendid adventure as well as

a magnificent achievement, since it involved traversing the Trakarding and Drolambao Glaciers and taking in, as well as the two peaks already mentioned, five summits east of the Drolambao Glacier. In the Ripimo their forays were also extensive, finding high passes at the head of both the Ripimo Shar Glacier — the Ripimo La (5,837m/19,150ft) and the Ripimo Nup into the Drogpa Nagtsang at the southern foot of Menlungtse (7,181m/23,560ft).

Alas, that kind of lightweight and free-ranging expedition is no longer possible in quite the same way in Nepal, and (for most of this decade) impossible in Rolwaling, closed, apparently without reason, in the early 1980s, but now at last reopened.

The real gem of Rolwaling, visible from afar, is Gauri Shankar (7,146m/23,440ft), for a long time confused with Everest and thought to be the highest mountain in the world! Attempted in the 1950s by a Swiss expedition led by Raymond Lambert, it was pronounced 'impossible'. In 1964 a British Expedition (really

133

Chortens on the road to Rolwaling.

a Rock and Ice team), led by Don Whillans and including Dennis Gray, Ian (Pin) Howell and Des Hadlum, got to 6,700m (22,000ft) before death by avalanche seemed a distinct possibility and retreat a sensible option. For a long time it remained one of the great mountain objectives, one of the few unclimbed 7,000ers left. In the end it fell to a joint American-Nepalese expedition, with John Roskelly and Dorje Sherpa from Solu taking the honours.

Numerous possible reasons for its closure have been put forward, one being that the route over the Tesi Lapcha is too dangerous for normal trekking groups and really only suitable for mountaineers. Undoubtedly, the route between Tsho Rolpo along the moraines of the Trakarding Glacier was dangerous and exposed to stonefall — several porters have been killed along this section. The other suggested reason, and the most likely, was that some trekkers/climbers used this remote valley close to the border as a way of crossing into Tibet to make illegal ascents. Although access to and through Rolwaling was forbidden, it was possible to climb on peaks such as Pacharmo by approaching the Tesi Lapcha from Namche Bazar and Thame, whilst the other official trekking peak, Ramdung, first climbed by Murray's party, could be approached from the south.

The trek through the narrow ravine of the Rolwaling Chhu has at last been reopened, and the small Sherpa enclave centred on Beding and Nagaon is no longer locked in splendid isolation. It will be a fascinating place to visit now this is possible, if only to see how traditional Sherpa culture, relatively unaffected by Western influence, has fared.

Dhaula Himal: . . . positively monstrous, several miles high without interruption, rather like the North Face of the Matterhorn, which isn't exactly inviting either, but this particular fiend is three times as big.
Gaston Rebuffat

Standing on Poon Hill in the cold half-light of morning has become a trekker's ritual. From the lodges at Ghorapani Deorali (alas, now being built almost to the top of the hill), duvet-clad figures puff the few hundred feet through straggling rhododendrons to wait like druids for sunrise. A cold wind always seems to blow before it does. Slowly the sky lightens as the fingers of the sun, not red or simply orange, but tinged with green and blue and crimson, grasp the sky from behind the standing stone of Machhapuchhare, to put colour into the day. It's difficult not to be hypnotized by the point on the horizon where the shafts of light converge, and watch the sun's sudden haste as it leaps the distant hills into the blue vault of sky.

But if you can turn your back on that and look across the purple void of the Kali Gandaki, what in the dark was a distant ghostly silhouette now appears the object of the sun's chase. Dhaulagiri (8,167m/26,795ft), in contrast to the inky ravine, is brilliant. Its south face, a huge amphitheatre of pleated ice and terminated buttresses, reflects the colours of sunrise. The mountain's mass is vast, but balanced by Tukuche Peak, whose steeply-tilted strata thrust upwards from the Kali. This glistening face of the mountain, seen across the 'deepest valley in the world', and about which Rebuffat's words were spoken, is almost 4,270m (14,000ft) high.

'Dhaulagiri' translates as 'the White Mountain' — a Himalayan Mont Blanc — but to mountaineers it has developed a reputation for difficulty and danger which belies its benign name. In a single tragedy during an American expedition in 1969, seven lives were lost during an attempt on the South East Ridge. In sixteen expeditions up to 1978, only four were successful, with a total of sixteen lives lost. Not without cause did the leader of the Austrian expedition in 1959 call Dhaulagiri 'the mountain without pity'. In 1960 a Swiss expedition, led by Max Eiselin and including Austrian Kurt Diemberger, was able to build on the experiences of past attempts in order to reach the summit. The expedition made assiduous use of the Pilatus-Porter single-engine aircraft to establish high camps, and carry loads and climbers to an Advanced Base Camp on the North East Col at 5,700m (18,700ft). The craft eventually crashed on take-off and had to be abandoned on Dambush Col!

But Dhaulagiri doesn't stand alone like an isolated giant. It is part of a great massif that includes no fewer than fifteen 7,000m summits, forming a serrated skyline that extends westwards from the Kali Gandaki for forty miles to Putha Hiunchuli (7,246m/23,773ft). Besides Dhaulagiri 1, there are five other peaks with the same name, of which Dhaulagiri 4 has a most tragic history. In all there were eight attempts on it before its ascent in 1975 by Japanese

climbers Kawazu and Yusada, who were lost during the descent. Their 'success' had been paid for, not only with their own lives, but with those of fourteen others killed on previous expeditions. The first major summit to be climbed in the range was Putha Hiunchuli — in 1954, Jimmy Roberts on leave from the Army, and Ang Nyima Sherpa made the top.

The frustrating thing about the Dhaulagiri Himal is that many of its peaks are on the 'permitted list', which means of course that climbing parties can trek in and around the area to establish their base camps. However, the expense of an expedition is prohibitive if all you want to do is walk what is an outstanding 'circuit' around the Dhaulagiri massif.

For the adventurous mountain wanderer there are really two such treks to be made in and around the range. I'm sure, however, that with a bit more mountaineering, similar to that performed in Rolwaling during the 'Golden Age' from 1950–1960, wonderful journeys could be pioneered. One of my journeys is the Dhaula Himal's equivalent of the circuit of Annapurna, only much more remote and demanding. In all the trek takes at least a month to complete, beginning and ending in Pokhara. The second of the two is a shorter sharper 'circuit' of Tukuche Peak and Dhaulagiri 1, following a route pioneered initially by Herzog's French Expedition of 1950, but in fact completed by the Academic Alpine Club of Zurich's expedition under the leadership of Bernhard Lauterberg. It was a strong team that included Andre Roche, and their reconnaissance did much to help the Swiss success of 1960.

Herzog's expedition of 1950 had a star-studded cast that included, along with Rebuffat, two other outstanding Chamonix guides — Lionel Terray and Louis Lachenal. Their approach from Pokhara was up the Kali Gandaki to Tukuche village. Trying to approach the mountain from its northern side, (the south was blatantly out of the question), they followed the true left flank of the Dhampus Khola north-west around Tukuche. Crossing the watershed at Dhampus Pass between Tukuche and Thapa Peak (6,012m/19,724ft), the way led them into an area which they called the 'Hidden Valley'; this in fact connects northwards with the Keha Lungpa, and is said to be the habitat for *tahr*, musk deer and snow leopard. Following the valley upstream, they finally crossed a pass on the ridge between Tukuche Peak (6,920m/22,703ft) and Sita Chuchura (6,639m/21,781ft), from where they at last glimpsed the north-east flank of their mountain, separated from them by a massive jumble of glaciers. This pass has subsequently been called French Pass (5,360m/17,585ft). They retreated from Dhaulagiri and eventually went on, once they had found it, to climb Annapurna 1 — the first 8,000er to fall.

The Austrians, on the other hand, arrived at the same spot but from a different direction and so pieced together what is an outstanding route, albeit quite a difficult one, around the mountain. From Pokhara they followed the trade route into the Kali Gandaki, leaving it at Beni (670m/2,198ft), once the winter watering hole of the Malla rulers of Parbat. Malebam is thought to have built a palace there in 1697 but it fell into decline after the Ghurka victories of 1786. It is today the administrative centre for the Mayangdi District.

Leaving the Kali the Austrians headed west up the valley of the Mayangdi Khola, following the true left bank of the river. Today there are new suspension bridges that undoubtedly make the going easier, as would the hot-spring at Tatopani after the dusty hot tramp from Pokhara. Their approach so far had followed the main trade route between Beni and Dhorpatan, where there is now an airstrip. At Mura, where there are fine views towards Dhaulagiri, they followed the valley of the Mayangdi northwards towards Dhaulagiri, leaving behind the well-populated and highly-terraced hillsides on the southern flanks of the range. They undoubtedly had a difficult time in the upper valley, having to blaze a path through dense bamboo and build many bridges. Eventually, beyond Dobang, where the route follows the river (closely in places), they had fine views of the rocky west flank of Dhaulagiri.

The headwaters of the Mayangdi Khola, now little more than a mountain torrent, have cut a deep ravine beyond Puchhare. Lauterberg's party eventually established their Base Camp at the foot of the North-West Ridge and climbed to within 1,500ft of the summit. Retreating from the mountain, they continued their exploration over the Mayangdi Glacier, glimpsed from French Pass by Terray and Oudot. Its melt-waters form the Mayangdi Khola. From here they explored the North-East Col that was vital to success on the eventual ascent route. The normal base camp for the North-East Ridge is placed on the glacier, one day's march above Pakabon campsite amongst the grass and gravel of an ablation valley.

Base Camp (4,750m/15,583ft) itself is in a sensational situation beneath the towering North Face of Dhaulagiri and the icefall tumbling from the North-East Col. The rest of the Dhaula Himal extends westwards with the peaks of Dhaulagiri 2 (7,751m/25,430ft), Dhaulagiri 3 (7,715m/25,312ft) and Dhaulagiri 5 (7,618m/24,993ft) commanding the attention.

From Base Camp the French Pass is only a few hours' hike away. By crossing the debris-covered glacier, the slopes of Sita Chuchura above the true right bank can be followed to lead to snow slopes beneath the pass. From its snowy summit the views to the north-east are of the 'Hidden Valley', and the surrounding summits of Tashi Kang and the Mukut Himal, from where the route of the French can be followed back to Tukuche in the Kali Gandaki.

The other route about which I dream and which

I long to traverse is the 'Grand Circuit' of the Dhaula Himal — certainly a journey of contrasts by all accounts. It doesn't penetrate so deeply into the heart of the mountains as does the 'climbers' route but neither does it stand back from the action like a viewer at an art gallery. Instead it's like a generous banquet at which you can take your fill of the best things on offer.

It begins by following the same route from Pokhara along the southern flank of the Dhaulagiris, continuing through terraced farmland to Dhorpatan. I always feel that once beyond the Kali Gandaki I'm in West Nepal. There is an airstrip at Dhorpatan and it might be possible to arrange a flight; certainly it would be possible to organize porters locally. My own preference would be for hillmen or Tibetans because now the route climbs northwards at the western margin of the massif through a scarcely populated region, crossing the main chain at the Jangla Bhanjyang (4,523m/14,839ft), where the views northwards are of Forbidden Dolpo and the Kanjiroba Himal.

This is Bhote country and the houses, as in Manang and other rain-shadow areas, indicate you have crossed the Greater Himalaya, reflecting the climate of the land and the cultural influence of Tibet. The descent from the pass leads to Tarakot (2,600m/8,530ft), where the houses are distinctly Tibetan, for now the route lies eastwards along the main Jumla—Jomosom trail, following the valley of the Barbung Khola (Bheri). This is considered the southern boundary of Dolpo. From Tarengaon the trail climbs out of the Barbung, turns sharply north and follows the Mukut

Looking towards the eastern end of the Dhaula Himal from the Tibetan fortress-style town of Jharkot. From here, roads lead north into Mustang or west to the Sangda La and the southern boundary of Dolpo.

Khola, crossing the Mul La (5,547m/18,200ft) and then the Sangda La (5,124m/16,810ft), before descending to Sangda and the profound gorge of the Keha Lungpa. Leaving the valley, the path then skirts the eastern end of the Dhaulagiri Himal, traversing the flank of Tashi Kang to Dangar Dzong, before descending to Jomosom and the Kali Gandaki.

But for the moment the route must remain an object of desire — something to dream about and save for the future. This is exactly how it is with Dolpo, now a National Park. Although it was made famous by Peter Matthiessen's popular book *The Snow Leopard*, it was really Buddhist scholar David Snellgrove in his book *Himalayan Pilgrimage* who highlighted this pocket of truly Tibetan culture with a mixture of Buddhism and the more ancient Bon Po religion. Perhaps even Dolpo will one day be open to careful travellers.

ROLWALING TREK

ITINERARY:

DAYS 1 – 4: KATHMANDU TO GONGAR

By road to Barabise. Cross Ghote Khosi then via Sun Khosi bazaar, upstream to Gortali. Follow main trail north-east to Dolangsa. Climb through rhododendrons and kharka to Dhumtali. Cross Tinsang La with views of Rolwaling peaks. Pass Bigu Gompa then on to Bulung and Bhote Kosi Valley.

DAYS 5 – 6: GONGAR TO SHAKPA

Continue north up valley. Cross suspension bridge at Chhechet and climb steeply to Simagaon. Ascend through rhododendrons to ridge crest and huts at Shakpa.

DAYS 7 – 8: SHAKPA TO BEDING

Now in Rolwaling Valley and a different landscape. Cross Daldung La and descend to Rolwaling Valley. Traverse Samba Danda through Sherpa settlements to Beding.

DAYS 9 – 14: BEDING TO NAMCHE BAZAR

Continue east up valley through magnificent wild scenery to Tsho Rolpo. Traverse moraine on north side of valley to snout of Drolambao Glacier. Climb ice near centre. Avoid route on Schneider map. Camp on glacier below slopes leading to Tesi Lapcha. Climb to pass and either camp just below crest or descent to

A Magar woman and child on the trek towards Dhorpatan.

In Dolpo — Bon po and traditional Tibetan Buddhism walk side by side, much the same as in Ladakh.

Ngole. Continue descending through Thengpo, Thame to Namche.

Further **2 days to Lukhla** with porters.

DIFFICULTY:

A long and arduous route with time at high altitude and a difficult and dangerous pass to cross. Really only suitable for mountaineers or a strong party with basic mountaineering skills. Traverse of Tsho Rolpo to glacier snout has rockfall dangers.

LOGISTICS:

Suitable only for self-sufficient parties. Local foods available en route. Nothing between Beding and Thame. Best to employ local porters in Rolwaling.

MAP:

General planning best done on Mandala Kathmandu/Lamasangu/Everest sheet. For detail use Schneider map, Rolwaling and Khumbu sheets 1:50,000.

DHAULAGIRI TREKS

It is possible to traverse the routes in either direction. My own choice would be an anti-clockwise circuit.

ITINERARY: MAYANGDI KHOLA AND FRENCH PASS

DAYS 1 – 3: POKHARA TO BENI
Through well-cultivated lowland via Naudanda, Daudari Dhara and Thamajung, Kusma, Baglung to Beni. This is hot walking pre- or post-monsoon. Large bazaar at Baglung for supplies.

DAYS 4 – 6: BENI TO PHALAI GAON
Leave the Kali Gandaki for the Mayangdi Khola. Depending on season, path follows either a high or low route. From Phedi climb steeply then steadily to Phalai Gaon.

DAYS 7 – 11: PHALAI GAON TO PAKABON
Turn northwards up the main valley leaving the Dhorpatan trail. Climb through scattered settlements and kharka. Cross a small glacier below Dhaulagiri to a melt-water valley at Pakabon.

DAYS 12 – 13: PAKABON TO BASE CAMP
The route follows moraines then climbs high above the ravine of the Mayangdi. Descending to the floor it then reaches the Mayangdi Glacier. Follow the glacier into its gorge, taking the true right bank into the valley leading towards French Pass.

DAYS 14—17: BASE CAMP TO TUKUCHE

Ascend snow slopes without difficulty to French Pass, then descend into Hidden Valley. Climb to Dhampus La and descend a rocky ridge, staying high above the Dhampus Khola. Descend through herders' huts to Tukuche. This route is poorly defined high up.

Return to Pokhara on the normal Annapurna route, or it is possible to fly from Jomosom. The trek to Pokhara takes 5—6 days.

DIFFICULTY:

A difficult and strenuous trek, requiring some technical skills to cross the glacier and climb snow slopes. The way is poorly defined and the paths in places precipitous. Poor weather in the higher sections would be particularly serious.

LOGISTICS:

Fly/drive to Pokhara. Porters available in Pokhara. Everyone needs to be well equipped for the crossing of Mayangdi Glacier and French Pass. It would be possible to fly to Jomosom, but it is then difficult to acclimatize before crossing the passes. Food and fuel would be needed for the section between Mura and Tukuche.

EQUIPMENT:

Conditions range from sub-tropical to arctic, so you need to carry suitable clothing for both, as well as ice-axes, crampons and ropes. Baglung has the last bazaar.

(Left) Tibetan culture and Khampas like this dominate much of the Forbidden Kingdom, especially north of the Himalaya in regions like Dolpo, Mustang, and the Na and Shar Kholas.

SEASON:

April/May, although it would be difficult in early April if there was a lot of snow. Post-monsoon, although colder would be ideal.

MAPS:

Mandala Jomosom to Jumla and Surkhet sheet, 1in to 4 miles.

DHAULAGIRI GRAND CIRCLE

ITINERARY:

DAYS 1—6: FOLLOW THE ABOVE ROUTE TO PHALAI GAON

DAY 7: PHALAI GAON TO DHORPATAN

Beyond Mura climb steeply through forest to Jalja La, which separates the drainage of the Kanali and Kali Gandaki. Continue westwards to Dhorpatan.

DAYS 8—13: DHORPATAN TO TARANKOT (DZONG)

Wild country leads eventually to the Jang La. Descend towards Barbung Khola and Tarakot, within the arid rain-shadow of the Himalaya and the southern boundary of Dolpo.

DAYS 14—17: TARAKOT TO MUKUT

Follow the Barbung eastwards through scattered villages to Tareng. Climb north-east to Mukut.

DAYS 18—22: MUKUT TO JOMOSOM

Cross to Mukut La and Sangda La. Descend Keha Lungpa traversing southern flank of Tashi Kang into Kali Gandaki valley. Descend to Jomosom and main trail.

'Rather would I dwell in some patched tent through which the winds blow than
in some lofty castle.' *Maysun, wife of Caliph Melawiya — seventh century.*

It normally takes six days from Jomosom to Pokhara.

DIFFICULTY:

A long trek through remote and difficult country. The passes are potentially dangerous in poor weather, although not difficult in ideal conditions. There may be route-finding problems between Dhorpatan and Tarakot. This trek is suitable only for experienced mountain walkers.

MAP:

Mandala Jomosom to Jumla and Surkhet sheet, 1in to 4 miles.

Gone Trekking:
How and when

Trekking in Nepal could hardly be simpler. There are few rules and regulations governing it, other than the need for a valid passport, a visa and a Trekking Permit for your chosen area.

VISA

These are available direct from the Nepalese Embassy or consulates in all countries where they have representation, and simply require you to do a bit of form filling, provide two passport photos and pay a small fee. However, you can arrive at the airport in Kathmandu or at the border and get a seven-day visa on the spot, which you can then have extended. If you are applying early by post, make sure that it covers the period you intend to be in Nepal!

TREKKING PERMIT

These are available in Kathmandu and are issued by the Central Immigration Office of the Home and Panchyat Ministry at Maiti Devi near Dilli Bazar. Again, photographs are required. You can also get permits in Pokhara for treks in the Annapurna region. This is especially useful for those entering Nepal from India.

HOW TO GO

There are many ways to go on a trek in Nepal. You can pre-book on an organized trek through a travel agent at home, organize your own trek through an agent in Nepal, or go it alone. At the end of the day it is a matter of personal style and money. Undoubtedly the services of a travel agent and the leading agencies do not come cheap, but by and large they do come trouble-free.

Commercial Treks

Most people work directly through an 'Adventure Travel' agent and simply book their passage on the trip of their choice. This means in most cases that, apart from having jabs, filling in a few forms, and packing bags, everything is taken care of for them. The agents provide, through their outfitters in Nepal, transfers to and from airport and hotel in Kathmandu, along with transfers to and from the start of the trek. They provide a 'Sherpa' crew, invariably including a Sirdar (headman) who acts as guide and looks after all organization on trek, and works closely with others who cook and carry to try to make it a trouble-free trip. In the best agencies helpers are trained in their various tasks, so that food cooked in camp, for instance, is of a high standard and as varied as possible to cater for Western tastes. The Sirdar will also take care of the hiring and payment of porters and the agency takes care of porter and staff insurance. In a few cases the agencies might provide a Western trip leader, whose primary function is to entertain the clients or act as a buffer between cultures, unless of course he is a specialist or a climbing leader.

As well as taking care of all the organization and red tape, the agencies make sure that things happen within a given time-frame; that destinations are reached and deadlines met. For those with a limited amount of time, agencies represent an ideal way to travel since no time is wasted in the mundane matters of organization. They also make it possible to visit many areas not served by lodges, allowing you to travel 'off the beaten trek', and to enjoy the wilder areas of Nepal. On the other hand, commercial treks tend to be more expensive. Many travel agents will also tailor-make a trip for individuals and groups.

The other important thing to remember is that agencies also provide all the equipment you will need, apart from personal clothes. Tents, cooking equipment, a dining tent, chairs, warm clothing on high treks for porters, sleeping mattresses, and in many cases sleeping bags and liners will all be included.

Agencies

It is possible to work directly through an agency in Nepal, buying from them the services you require. It might be that you want their services in full — this will hardly differ from a commercial trek. On the other hand, you might simply want them to provide a Sirdar, a cook and perhaps some equipment, and look after the other matters, such as buying food, getting permits and paying porters, yourself. This does give you a great deal of freedom and, for those with the time and inclination to do it, there is the enjoyment of organizing an expedition.

Going it Alone

Many people simply opt to arrive in Kathmandu and go off on trek in much the same way as you hike at the weekend at home. Undoubtedly trekking has come a long way since Jimmy Roberts organized the first treks in Nepal. On many of the classic treks, lodges, both simple and sophisticated, pepper the trail, offering every kind of delight from pancakes and pizza to yak burgers and apple pie — some of them even offer Nepali food! Thus it's possible (and popular), armed with a trekking permit, to hike many of the 'classic treks' simply with a backpack. The ways are easy to follow and there are few dangers, although there have been several instances recently where solo trekkers, in particular women, have been robbed or have vanished.

You can of course take a tent and stove, hire a few porters and take off into the more remote areas. Just about everything is possible in Nepal. However, in some areas, like the recently opened Kangchenjunga, solo trekkers relying on local lodges are not allowed, and only organized, self-contained trekking parties are permitted. Trekking light and using the lodges is certainly the cheapest way to go. In most cases you would be hard-put to spend more than £10 per day, whereas a commercial trek would be nearer £50.

TRANSPORT

Apart from the roads linking the main cities, Nepal and the combustion engine have yet to get to grips with one another. In the medieval streets of Kathmandu however, the situation is getting out of hand. Taxis are readily available, mostly with working meters; if not, agree a price before you travel, and be willing to argue. Bicycle rickshaws are also available in town and these are very cheap, as are the scooter taxis. Bicycles are available for hire in Kathmandu and Pokhara, are very cheap and are a great way to get around.

Buses

Local buses are the cheapest method of travel and can be a social and physical adventure.

ExplorAsia

The Pioneers of Himalayan Adventure Travel

- Trekking and climbing with Mountain Travel
- Tiger Tops Jungle Lodge
- Wildlife Safaris
- River Running
- Fishing
- Cultural Tours

ExplorAsia are the experts in Nepal, India, Kashmir, Ladakh.
Contact us for further details or ask for a copy of our superb new brochure.

ExplorAsia Limited
13 Chapter Street   London SW1P 4NY
Telephone 01-630 7102   Telex 266774 EXPLOR G   Fax 01-630 0355

They have a content that is animal, vegetable and mineral in aroma and texture. There are also 'de-luxe' buses that ply the same routes — these are more expensive and not quite so adventurous.

Most of the services leave from the main bus station on the east side of the Tundhikhel parade ground. The Trisuli bus leaves from Pakanajol, west of Thamel, whilst the Pokhara service leaves from outside the main post office.

Flying

Many trekking areas are served by STOL airstrips that provide the quickest way in and out of those areas. Nepal's airline (RNAC), despite all the stories trekkers like to tell, is first class, given that much of the flying must be 'seat of the pants' stuff. Certainly, some of the airstrips do make for steep, rough walking, let alone landings. The real problems with local flying in Nepal are the vagaries of the weather, coupled with too great a demand on too few aircraft. Lukhla in particular is a bad place to be when the weather closes in. People on a tight schedule should think twice about flying in and out of such a place.

PORTERS

In Nepal porters are the haulage system of the country. On a commercially organized trek their hiring is done by the Sirdar. Although porters are invariably in all of the main centres, and it is frequently possible to get someone to porter from a village along the way, they often become scarce during the main trekking season or when crops have to be planted. For example, during April in the Khumbu, when the staple food of potatoes has to be planted, it is usually a difficult business.

Remember that you are responsible for your porters' well-being on trek, especially if you

want them to go into remote areas. On high treks above the snowline you must make sure they are adequately clothed. By our standards they are usually tough, but if you neglect them you should expect trouble.

HIMALAYAN CLIMBING

Many of the journeys described in this book were done in order to get to and from a mountain. Indeed, trekking has often been described as the enjoyable bit of an expedition. Climbing in Nepal is, by and large, a complicated and expensive affair. Of all the mountains in Nepal, only 104 peaks are on the permitted list, and a long wait exists for the better-known peaks as well as a hefty booking fee.

Apart from the Expedition Peaks, there was created in 1978 under the control of the newly-formed Nepal Mountaineering Association (NMA), a list of 18 mountains, between 5,587m (18,330ft) and 6,654m (21,830ft), called 'Trekking Peaks'. These can be climbed without the problem of the financially restricting and administratively onerous regulations governing Expedition Peaks. With little more expense and red tape than is required for trekking, you too can attempt a Himalayan mountain.

SEASONS AND WEATHER

There is always somewhere to go and something to do in Nepal, whatever the weather. During the summer monsoon months, between July and September, the flowers in the mountains are glorious. This is a time when Sherpas return to a more traditional lifestyle, taking their animals to the high pastures that have become rich in feed. Few tourists see this. Treks beyond the Greater Himalaya in regions like Manang would also be possible, since these places sit in a rain-shadow; however, to get there you would need to be a lover of leeches!

Most travellers and trekking companies think of Nepal as having two major seasons. The first is the pre-monsoon period, or spring, that extends from late March to the end of May. With the colder winter months over, temperatures gradually increase so that treks beginning at low altitudes, out of Pokhara for instance, can be very hot indeed — perhaps in excess of 38°C (100°F). Days can become hazy, with the distant views obscured, and clouds are a common feature of the afternoons. Sudden snowfall at this time (not uncommon in March and April) soon burns off, and both the days and nights are getting warmer. The real treat in the spring months are the flowers, especially the rhododendrons. You must be careful early in the pre-monsoon period that passes and ridges are not blocked with snow and footpaths impassable.

By late September, when the monsoon ends, the days become crystal clear. This is the real feature of the autumn and winter months. The mornings and especially the evenings can feel particularly brisk, but in sunshine the conditions are ideal for trekking. Typical mid-November temperatures at lower altitudes range between 38°C (100°F) in the sun and 16°C (60°F) in the shade, with night-time minimums of 16°C (60°F). At higher altitudes midday sun/shade temperatures range from 9°C (48°F) to −5°C (24°F) with night-time temperatures of −11°C (13°F) not uncommon. Sudden storms will leave snow high up and on north-facing slopes this will remain, often unconsolidated.

A DAY ON A TRADITIONAL TREK

A typical day for a self-contained party on an organized trek is very much as follows.

Your day begins at dawn when the kitchen boy calls through the tent, 'Bed tea, Sahib.'

A mug of hot sweet tea is my favourite brew in Nepal, and after this pleasure it's time to get up. On the best-run treks there might also be a bowl of washing water! Before breakfast you should pack up your things. Whatever you think you will need that day — camera, spare sweater, notebook, water/wind proofs — should be packed into your own rucksack and the rest should go into your kitbag so that the porters can get going as soon as possible, and the camp can be taken down.

Breakfast on most commercial treks is fairly simple — oatmeal, or some other kind of cereal, biscuits and hot drinks. This is a good time to fill your water bottle for the day and add the iodine.

There follows three or four hours' walking. The cook and kitchen boy have gone ahead to a known destination and prepared lunch. Many trekkers agree that this is the best meal of the day — often chapattis, pancakes, perhaps fried eggs and potatoes, and again plenty of drinks. This 'brunch' is taken around midday, perhaps a little earlier, and I try to arrange it near a stream where we can wash clothes and ourselves. On some treks, especially those out of Pokhara, it's good to find shade from the sub-tropical sun at the hottest part of the day. Again, this is a good time to fill up the water bottle.

In the afternoon another three or four hours brings you to camp. The Sherpa crew usually supervise that and by the time you arrive things will be happening, including, hopefully, a brew of hot sweet tea! At this point you will have the opportunity to explore a local village or simply to stand still and relax. After all, trekking is really a holiday and a chance for you to see and explore Nepal.

Dinner is usually served between six and seven and is invariably soup, followed by rice and vegetable or meat curry, and perhaps some fresh or tinned fruit. Most of the trekking outfitters have an amazingly similar menu and routine. The only variants are the standard of the cooking and of course the hygiene.

Most trekking days vary in length between five and eight hours, although from time to time they can be longer. Day stages are usually dictated by porters, who know exactly how far a group can go. Sometimes this is affected by the availability of campsites or lodges, and at other times the view or a particular place of interest might create a diversion.

This kind of trekking is very relaxed, giving plenty of time to enjoy the scenery, the villages and people. Keen photographers will spend time chasing after pictures, whilst others can sketch, write, read or simply stand and stare.

INDEPENDENT TREKKERS

For those travelling independently, using the lodges, the day also has a structure. The availability of lodges will obviously determine where you stay and what treks you can do, although it is still possible for a small group to find accommodation in a private house in some areas, and to share the family's food.

The average lodge provides dormitory accommodation, usually on a wooden platform. You would be expected to have your own mattress and sleeping bag. Some of the 'up-market' ones have private rooms, offer an extensive menu and even have hot showers.

Tea and drinks are usually always available. On the other hand, food can be a long time coming. In many lodges I've used, especially those that are busy and offer a wide variety of dishes, several hours have sometimes passed before the food has arrived. In the evening, unless you are ravenous or dog-tired it doesn't really matter; you can have another brew and talk with other trekkers, and there is always the trekker's best friend — Nepali glucose biscuits — to sustain you. On the other hand, in the

mornings or at lunch-time, when you want to get going it can be frustrating to wait an hour or so for something that takes five minutes to eat. There is no easy solution, other than ordering simple dishes like *dhalbhaat*, eating plenty of biscuits, or not being in a hurry! Having said this, there are some lodges where the service is expeditious.

Many independent travellers in Nepal carry their own backpack, and employ a porter to carry part of their load. Some of these are simply porters whilst others act almost as Sirdars, able to organize food and lodging, route-find and much more. In my experience this is a very enjoyable way to travel.

The way to travel further in Nepal is not to rush it but simply spend more hours of the day walking. This is a luxury that the independent traveller has over the organized group, where porter stages to a great extent dictate the length of day. On the other hand, the campers can stop, by and large, where they want and travel beyond habitation into the remoter areas.

EQUIPMENT

Most people on trek for the first time invariably take too much equipment. Only those who have to carry it themselves refine their needs to what they can stuff into a rucksack, shorten the handle of their toothbrush, and dispose of cutlery in favour of a single spoon! If you are going on a traditional trek, with its bandabhast of Sherpas and porters, there is a temptation to add just another couple of T-shirts and an extra sweater — just in case. Fortunately, the 20kg limit on most airlines is a deterrent to most of us.

There is no definitive equipment list. Each trek is like the seasons — different. Altitude, difficulty and length all impose requirements and any perfect list would have to relate to a specific trek and season. A trek to the Khumbu, for example, in November, intending to cross

DESCENDING FROM AMA DABLAM. TAWECHE BEYOND. PHOTO: BILL O'CONNOR.

EQUIPMENT *for* ADVENTURE

KARRIMOR RUCSACS, CLOTHING AND SLEEPING BAGS ARE WORLD RENOWNED FOR THEIR TECHNICAL EXCELLENCE, QUALITY, AND CARRYING COMFORT.

SINCE 1958 KARRIMOR HAS SUPPLIED EQUIPMENT TO MANY LEADING INTERNATIONAL EXPEDITIONS, INCLUDING SUCCESSFUL ASCENTS OF EVEREST, AND THE FIRST WINTER K2 EXPEDITION. KARRIMOR PRODUCTS ARE NOW AVAILABLE IN OVER 20 COUNTRIES WORLDWIDE.

KARRIMOR INTERNATIONAL LTD,
PETRE ROAD, CLAYTON-LE-MOORS, ACCRINGTON, LANCASHIRE. BB5 5JP

the Tsho La or Mingbo, can expect many cold mornings and nights, the possibility of winds and the need to cross a lot of snow and ice. On the other hand, wandering up to Muktinath or through Helambu in the spring, when the days are hot and where the altitudes are never great, you can get away with less and lighter gear. However, there *are* some basics and advice on those should prove useful.

Kit Bags

The best way to pack equipment for porters to carry is in an army-style kit bag or zippered holdall. Porters string two or more of these together and carry them on a tump line or headstrap (*namlo*). My own preference is for the holdall rather than the military-style bag, because of the ease of access. Fitting a padlock is also sensible to prevent pilfering. I personally like to pack all my things in coloured stuff sacks inside the bag; this not only keeps them clean and dry but also makes packing simple.

Clothing on Trek

For trekking you don't need a lot of specialist equipment, indeed, most porters wear little more than a cotton shirt and trousers or loin cloth, and perhaps a pair of flip-flops or basketball boots!

For Westerners the choice is wider. Light cotton trousers or loose skirt or shorts, with a t-shirt and a pair of running shoes or lightweight boots is the norm on most treks. In the morning or early evening this might be supplemented by a fleece sweater and pants, or perhaps a light down jacket or vest. These can be put into your rucksack later as the day warms up.

It's usually only on the higher treks or between November and January that wool shirts and thermal underwear become necessary. Unless it is overcast or windy, the day is usually warm, but the early mornings and the evenings

can be very cold so, unless you want to retire early to your sleeping bag, take warm clothing, a down parka, gloves and a wool hat.

Boots

If you have a favourite pair of comfortable walking boots, stick with them. If you are looking for a pair for the first time, ask yourself the following: will I be going above the snowline, or on very rough and rocky terrain, and will I need to fit crampons? If the answer is yes to all of these, then you need boots with a very different specification from those of someone doing a low-level trek below the snowline with nothing technical involved.

Modern lightweight boots have revolutionized hill-walking for the beginner. No longer is it necessary to spend months breaking a boot in, indeed, many need hardly any treatment at all. Fabric upper boots, although generally less durable or waterproof than leather boots, are ideal for normal trekking where you encounter little rain. They also have the added advantage of allowing the foot to breathe.

Vibram-style soles are a definite advantage, especially on muddy or rough trails where they provide a good grip and cushion the foot. Those intending to climb will probably be familiar with lightweight plastic mountain boots which have all but replaced leather boots, and know how uncomfortable they are for normal hiking.

Many lightweight boots are too flexible to take a crampon. A specialist retailer should be able to advise you on the most suitable boot once he knows your plans.

Shell Clothing

A windproof and waterproof shell is essential for all but the shortest and lowest treks. You may never take them out of your rucksack but, should you get caught out in a sudden storm on an exposed ridge, they can prove a life-saver. Even a moderate breeze on the top of Kala Pattar or Gokyo Ri can be withering, and a windproof layer will make it bearable and perhaps even enjoyable. Modern fabrics like Gore-tex and Sympatex which are breathable are much more comfortable to wear than PU-coated materials. My own preference is for trousers or salopettes with side zips that can easily be got on and off over boots, and I also like my jacket to be ventable. Being able to control the body's temperature is the most important rule in staying warm.

Layering Systems

In a country like Nepal, where altitudes on trek vary tremendously, and the day and night temperatures alternate between the extremes, and where there is the possibility of sudden changes in the weather, a clothing system that is highly functional and adaptable to conditions is essential. A system of clothing based on several light, warm layers, rather than a single bulky sweater over a wool shirt, is ideal. Fleece salopettes or tracksuit-style bottoms are perfect on cold days and around camp in the evening, and when combined with a 'shell layer', they become adaptable to any conditions – never too hot and hopefully never too cold. As much as I like fleece because of its lightness and warmth, I don't like synthetic material for the skin layer (for thermal underclothing, for example). On trek or expedition you end up wearing clothes longer than normal, and polypropolene smells (so everybody says). Use wool – not the itchy kind, but the comfortable and warm kind that can be worn for a long time without the polyprop-stink.

Rucksack

You do still see a number of independent trekkers carrying a traditional metal pack-frame suitable for heavier loads, but modern internal-frame packs are probably more comfortable and certainly more stable. If you are not intending to carry a heavy load, you should opt for the Alpine-style day pack with a simple internal frame like the Karrimor format, preferably with a hip belt. Many trekkers on commercial treks carry sacks that are too small and inevitably end up with half the things they need tied to the outside, looking like tinkers. A rucksack with a lid pocket and perhaps a couple of small outside pockets is useful for quick access to water bottle, maps, sun cream and guidebook.

Water Bottle

Do carry at least a 1-litre bottle. The plastic Nalgene bottles are ideal. You need to hydrate to go high, and you also need to drink much more than usual when trekking in the sub-tropical conditions out of Pokhara, for instance. Do remember to carry some iodine crystals or solution for water purification. Many trekkers now carry small ceramic water filters which are very good, but quite expensive.

Head Lamp

You need some kind of light in your tent at night and perhaps for an early start. A head lamp is far more useful than a hand lamp, since it leaves both hands free for whatever you are doing.

First Aid Kit

Most commercial treks have a first aid kit for the group. However, individuals should carry a basic personal first aid pack. After all, if the group kit is on the back of a porter, and he's two hours ahead when you need a plaster or a pill, it's not a lot of use. You should also know how to use it!

Equipment Check-List

I devised this list as an *aide-memoire* for both myself and for clients I've taken on trek and expedition. It doesn't represent what you must take, but rather aims to highlight some of the things you mustn't forget. If it doesn't list things vital to you, simply add them and make it your own definitive list.

On an organized trek you can disregard group equipment and invariably eating utensils and sleeping bag, unless of course you prefer your own 'tin mug' and rancid pit.

Boots and shoes:
Comfortable shoes for travelling and for city
Running shoes
Trekking boots
Climbing boots
Down boots

Mountaineering equipment (individual):
Harness
Crampons
Ice-axes
Crash hat
Head torch/batteries/bulbs
Ascenders
Descender

Gloves:
Lightweight thermal
Dachstein mitts or ski gloves
Overmitts
Silk liners

Headwear:
Sun hat
Ski hat
Balaclava

Socks:
Cotton athletic
Wool hiking

Gaiters:
Yeti-style
Ankle

Shirts:
Long-sleeved, and cotton
T-shirts

Underwear:
Regular
Thermal/long

Trousers:
Shorts
Long cotton hiking/skirt
Warm/climbing/breeches
Tracksuit/fleece

Sweaters:
Lightweight fleece or wool

Sleeping bag:
Down HA
Lightweight down or synthetic
Cotton liner
Gore-tex bivvi cover
Sleeping pad/Karrimat/Thermorest

Rucksack and kit bags:
Large capacity expedition
Alpine day sack
Heavy-duty kit bag/holdall
Small duffel for things in Kathmandu

Shell clothing:
Climbing jacket
Salopettes/trousers with full zips
Windsuit HA

Insulated clothing:
Ski jacket
Down parka
Down pants
Down vest

Bits and pieces:

Towel
Washing kit
Personal first aid
Repair kit
Sunglasses
Sun cream
Lip salve
Plastic bags
Altimeter
Compass
Binoculars
Maps
Notebook/pens/pencil
Camera gear/batteries/film
Toilet paper
Swimsuit
Reading material
Penknife
Wide-necked bottle
Stuff sacks
Marker pen
'Wet wipes'
Passport photos
Walkman/tapes

Eating utensils:

Cup/large capacity
Knife, fork, spoon
Plate
Bowl
Two 1-litre water bottles

Group equipment:

Tents
Ropes
Tapes/slings
Karabiners
Ice screws
Snow bars
Deadmen
Rock pegs
Nut rack/Friends
Cookers

Tower stove
Cooking pots
Medical box
Porter clothing
Dining tent/tarp
Sherpa kitchen
Pressure cooker
Water containers
Kerosene containers
Plastic containers for butter/oil/sugar
Plastic bags
Kerosene lamps
Repair kit
Camp stools/tables
Toilet tent (?)

MAPS

The adventurous trekker has much to be thankful for when it comes to maps of Nepal, for much is left to the imagination. The popular areas have maps to a reasonable scale, which give little excuse for getting lost, but it is quite understandable when a trekker gets the name of a mountain or village wrong, because even the maps can't agree about those!

Most maps are based on the original Survey of India, although many of the blue dyeline maps in the Mandala and Yeti Trekking series, often the only ones generally available, have been redrawn with a degree of artistic licence. The Survey of India was carried out between 1924–1927 to a scale of 1:63,360, whereas most of the Mandala maps are to a scale of 1:125,000 or 1:250,000. Place names can vary between editions and you must treat altitudes with caution — it's very depressing to spend all day sweating uphill, only to find that according to the map you are lower than when you started!

Some areas are covered by, larger-scale coloured sheets generally referred to as Schneider maps after Erwin Schneider the cartographer who supervised the field-work.

These maps, printed in Vienna by Kartographische Anstalt Freytag-Bernt unt Artaria to the scales of 1:50,000 and 1:25,000 with 40-metre contour intervals, are especially good for mountaineering use. Unfortunately, few areas are covered. From a trekking point of view, the most notable exception is the Annapurna Himal. Even so, the Schneider maps have some notable errors, and not just with peak or river names. In the Khumbu, for instance, Cholatse is called Jobo Lhaptsan and the Bhote Khosi called the Nangpo Tsangpo, both names that no local can remember using. It's worth noting that Bhote Kosi is hardly a suitable name either, since no part of the river actually drains Tibet. Perhaps Nangpo Khosi would be more accurate? More seriously, the 1987 Langtang map has left off major trails — like the one from Syabru into Langtang itself!

The Everest area, always commercially a good bet when it comes to making a new map, has recently been given the National Geographic treatment. Under the direction of Brad Washburn a 1:50,000 scale map has been produced, centred on Everest, using the latest in satellite and computer-aided technology. The result is a superb map of the area north of Pangboche, covering alas, only a small trekking area. It is interesting that this sheet, brought out in 1988, should have misnamed Kongma Tse, one of the listed trekking peaks. It calls it instead by its old name, Mehra, which was changed in 1983.

In 1977 an atlas entitled *Himalaya* was published by Gakushunkenkusha Ltd as part of the Mountaineering Maps of the World series, edited by Ichiro Yoshizawa. It provides some excellent detail to fill the gaps in existing maps.

HEALTH AND HAZARDS

Unlike Himalayan mountaineering, which has a morbid safety record, trekking in Nepal seems a safe and healthy pastime. That is, apart from the normal dangers inherent in high hills and travel in the Third World!

With precaution a few muscular aches and pains along with a mild bout of Kathmandu Quickstep should be all that most of us suffer. That said, the potential for sickness and injury is enormous: hepatitis, dysentery, cholera, malaria, meningitis and rabies are but a few of the nasties that come to mind, along with altitude-related ailments such as acute mountain sickness (AMS), pulmonary and cerebral oedema, snow-blindness, hypothermia and frostbite, or, alternatively, sunstroke. Or quite simply you can be nudged off the trail and down the hill by a passing yak.

Fortunately, considering the crowds who now trek in Nepal, many of whom are not normally mountain hikers, the number of serious accidents is thankfully small.

The scope of this book doesn't allow me to deal with the medical aspects of trekking and travel fully. Those wishing to cover the subject in depth should consult those books in the medical section of the reading list. In particular I have found James Wilkerson's book *Medicine for Mountaineers* first class.

Normal health precautions are essential before any long-haul travel, and more so with trekking holidays where you will be in remote places for much of the time and taking relatively strenuous exercise daily. So here are a few tips from a fellow traveller, albeit a healthy one, who has over the years had to treat more things than he cares to mention.

Fitness

If you really want to enjoy your trip, get fit before the trek not on the trek. Arriving in Nepal out of shape having taken no exercise for months, possibly years, is asking for trouble. Nepal, like life in general, is full of ups and downs. Run, walk, swim, bike, do circuits, whatever, but exercise *before* you go. You don't need to be marathon-fit, but you will enjoy it more if your legs have reasonable muscle tone and your heart-rate has got above its resting 90! A long trek with its ups, and especially its long downs, will sort out those with 'bad' knees. Wearing a knee support and taking anti-inflammatory drugs is one answer.

Feet

Foot problems, such as blisters, are largely a thing of the past with modern lightweight trekking boots, especially if you take time to break in your boots and toughen your feet. Normal foot hygiene also goes a long way to eliminating any problems. Many trekkers hike in training shoes which, although very comfortable, give little in the way of support. Hill-walking is a skill; if you haven't got it, a good pair of comfortable boots will go a long way towards making it more enjoyable.

Stomach

The talking point in many a trekkers' lodge and dining tent is Kathmandu Quickstep or, for those arriving from India, Delhi Belly. Those who haven't got it worry about catching it, and those who have it seem to want to share the experience. Most of the problems are caused through contaminated water and you have to accept that most of the water is not clean. Much of the contamination, according to local experts, seems to come from faeces. Water and sewage in Nepal seem to meet frequently and mix well, but unfortunately they and we don't. Not without cause did a stricken travelling companion refer to the sub-continent as the 'Turd World'. Not drinking the water unless you know it has been boiled and filtered, or has had iodine added, will go a long way to keeping you safe. Don't clean your teeth in your hotel with tap water and be careful of fruit drinks

made from squash mixed with untreated water. The lodges are a constant source of infection. Ideal standards of hygiene are impossible to maintain and ensure. After taking care of your own personal hygiene, you pays your money and you takes your chance. Cooked food doesn't seem to be the problem, and local food such as *dhalbaat* in most cases seems safe. Self-contained and commercial trekking groups, by and large, have more control over hygiene, and hot water for washing hands before meals or outside the toilet tent is a help. The cooks and staff of the leading agencies are also trained to maintain a reasonable standard of hygiene when cooking and washing up.

On the positive side, most cases of sickness or diarrhoea are short-lived, and the only treatment needed is to maintain liquid intake and to eat only simple foods like boiled rice. Giardia also seems to be quite common and is easily identifiable by the foul-smelling (rotten eggs) burps and farts it produces. Fortunately it responds quickly to a course of Bactrim. Re-hydration powder 'Jevanjal', available in small sachets in Kathmandu, is essential to the trekkers' first aid kit. Ciproxin appears to be the first antibiotic which has been found to be effective in treating travellers' diarrhoea. However, it is available only on prescription in Britain and should be taken two tablets twice a day for five days as soon as diarrhoea or sickness develop.

Whilst in Kathmandu it is certainly worth visiting the Himalayan Rescue Association (HRA) office near the Kathmandu Guest House in Thamel. They offer a great deal of help and advice, and Dr David Shlimm has produced a leaflet on 'Travellers' Diarrhoea' which is the best available.

Head, Heart and Altitude

After attacks on the stomach, altitude-related problems seem to be the next major concern or possible cause of difficulty for trekkers. Being in good shape definitely helps, but it is not a guarantee of a trouble-free trip. The greatest provocation is going too high too fast. Going to altitude slowly with adequate rest days coupled with good hydration seems to work for most people. For a few there is a definite altitude ceiling for which the cure seems to be simply to go down. Few treks take you higher than 5,500 metres and rarely for more than a day. However, some treks do stay above 5,000 metres for a considerable time and care needs to be taken once there and in getting there. Many trekkers seem to use Diamox (acetazolamide), which helps, but isn't as good as sound acclimatization. Be aware of the signs of altitude sickness — headaches, being out of breath, loss of appetite, nausea and dizziness are telling you it's time to stand still or to go down. Listen to your body and descend — things never get better going higher.

Trekkers'/Climbers' Cough

A Nepali dawn chorus is not the sweet trill of warblers on the bough, but a hacking cough and the raucous clearing of throats. It seems to be endemic amongst locals, and is the result, no doubt, of living in a dry, dust-laden atmosphere outside and a smoke-filled room inside — the effect is that of a nineteenth-century TB ward. A few days in the dust of Kathmandu, coupled with nights spent in smoky lodges, followed by some hard trekking and heavy breathing in the thin cold air of altitude, often results in sore throats and occasional respiratory infection. Once again, plenty of liquid and throat sweets to lubricate the tubes seem to help, whilst for those who are producing infected green phlegm, it's time for some antibiotics.

Red Eye

The dust-laden, smoke-filled atmosphere often also produces eye problems. Personal hygiene helps. Outside, bright sunlight and snow cause their own problems and good sun or snow glasses are the only answer.

Sunburn

This is a common and very painful problem often encountered on the first few days of a trek. Keen to be rid of the pallid complexion of a tourist, trekkers do not pay enough attention to protecting the skin against the roasting rays of a sub-tropical sun. Hiking out of Pokhara or Kathmandu can be like a furnace — the number of well-cooked trekkers you see glowing red and later peeling confirms this. The answer is quite simply to use the best sun screen and lip salve available. You will be outside most of the day, and there is plenty of time to tan.

Cold Injury

On most treks this should not be a problem, but beware, on those treks crossing high snowy passes such as the Thorong La, Tsho La and Mingbo La, it is a very real danger. Firstly, having inadequate footwear is likely to lead, on a pre-dawn start when crossing a pass, to frozen toes and possibly some frost nip. Being caught out in poor weather has certainly caused, in the case of badly-equipped trekkers and porters, hypothermia, frostbite and in some cases death. Being properly equipped and not taking a chance on a crossing in poor weather, especially with porters, is the best advice anyone can give.

Haemorrhoids

Although no one likes to own up to them, haemorrhoids seem to be quite common amongst back-packers and mountaineers, possibly the result of physical effort and the strain of carrying. Once again, hygiene seems to be the answer, and to that end (!), a box of 'wet wipes' carried in your rucksack and suppositories in the first aid kit will help.

Further Reading

In spite of the fact that Nepal only opened up her borders to mountaineers in 1949, this fascinating country has produced a wealth of words. Many of the early books written about Nepal provide intriguing reading, describing a medieval society that, despite the impact of the West, is still there today.

Of mountaineering books there are too many to list. In particular the Everest region has inspired enough books to fill a small library.

In Kathmandu are some of the best book shops I know, with books on all aspects of Nepal which are just not available elsewhere.

The selection below is personal — what I have found to be most useful on each subject.

Historical and General

Bernstein, Jeremy, *The Wildest Dreams of Kew* (Simon and Schuster, New York)
(Good historical material.)
Buchanan-Hamilton, Francis, *An Account of the Kingdom of Nepal* (London 1819)
Kirkpatrick, William, *An Account of the Kingdom of Nepaul* (London 1811)
Matthiesson, Peter, *The Snow Leopard* (Chatto and Windus)
(A spiritual journey into Dolpo with George Schaller.)

Guide Books

Armington, Stan, *Trekking in the Nepal Himalaya* (Lonely Planet)
(A good guide to the classic routes.)
Bezruchka, Stephen, *Trekking in Nepal* (Sahayoki Press/Cordee)
(The most comprehensive guide to classic treks with useful chapters on the country and its people.)
Fleming, Robert and Linda, *Kathmandu Valley* (Kandansha International, Tokyo)
Van Gruisen, Lisa, *Nepal: An Insight Guide* (APA Productions, Hong Kong)
(Beautifully illustrated general guide packed full of good information, but not about trekking.)
Nakano, Toru, *Trekking in Nepal* (Allied Press)

(Superb landscape pictures but terrible text. Reaches the parts the others leave out, including areas closed to trekkers.)
O'Connor, Bill, *Trekking Peaks of Nepal* (Crowood Press/Cloudcap, 1989)
(A comprehensive guide to Nepal's permitted Trekking Peaks and treks to the major areas, including details on organizing lightweight expeditions.)
Swift, Hugh, *Trekkers' Guide to the Himalaya and Karakoram* (Hodder and Stoughton)
(Good generally about trekking in Nepal.)

Adventure/Mountaineering

Bonington, Chris, *Annapurna South Face* (Caswell, London)
(Good expedition background for those visiting the Sanctuary.)
Bowman, W.E., *The Ascent of Rum Doodle* (Dark Peak, Sheffield)
(If, after reading numerous expedition accounts all written to the same formula, you can take no more, try this. It's about the world's highest peak, written in exactly the same formula, but in the vein of Monty Python. A ripping good yarn.)
Cleare, John, *World Guide to Mountains* (May Flower Books, London)
(Packed with facts about Nepal's mountains.)
Cleare, John, *Trekking, Great Walks of the World* (Unwin Hyman, 1988)
(Good chapter on the Annapurna Circuit.)
Herzog, Maurice, *Annapurna* (E.P. Dutton, New York)
(Epic account of the first 8,000-metre peak to be climbed. Classic.)
Hillary, Ed, *East of Everest* (Dutton, New York)
(Story of the New Zealand expedition to the Barun.)
Hunt, John, *The Ascent of Everest* (Hodder and Stoughton, London)
(Classic account of the first ascent.)
Murray, W.H., *The Scottish Himalayan Expedition* (Dent, London)
Noyce, Wilfrid, *The Fish's Tail*

(Account of the 1957 Machhapuchhare Expedition. Good information on The Sanctuary.)

Noyce, Wilfrid, *South Col* (Heinemann, London)

(A personal account of the 1953 Everest Expedition by one of the finest mountain writers of his generation.)

Rowell, Galen, *Many People Come, Looking, Looking* (The Mountaineers of Seattle)

(A beautifully illustrated book covering several expeditions to various parts of Asia.)

Shipton, Eric, *The Untravelled World* (Hodder and Stoughton, London)

(Republished by Diadem)

Tilman, H.W., *Nepal Himalaya* (Cambridge University Press)

(Good information on Langtang, Ganesh and Manang. Republished by Diadem/Mountaineers of Seattle as part of *Seven Mountain-Travel Books*.)

Natural History/Culture

Bista, Dor Bahandur, *People of Nepal* (Ratna Pustak Bhandur, Kathmandu)

(The best available on the subject.)

Fantini, Mario, *Mani Rimdu* (Toppan Co. Singapore)

(A well-illustrated picture book that goes some way to unfolding the mystery of this Sherpa dance drama.)

Fleming, Fleming and Bangdel, *Birds of Nepal* (Avalok, Kathmandu)

(The most comprehensive and lavishly illustrated field guide available.)

Furer-Haimendorf, Christoph, *Himalayan Traders* (John Murray, London)

(An academic but readable account of Bhote traders.)

Gurung, Harka, *Vignettes of Nepal* (Sahayogi Press, Nepal)

(Written by Nepal's premier geographer. Full of detailed information, facts and figures. Also a good read.)

Hagen, Toni, *Nepal: The Kingdom in the Himalaya* (Kummerley and Frey, Berne)

(First-rate chapters on geology, agriculture, climate and so on. One of the best books available on Nepal generally. Essential reading.)

Polunin and Stanton, *Flowers of the Himalaya* (Oxford University Press, London)

(Polunin was with Tilman in 1949 in Langtang.)

Schaller, George B., *Stones of Silence* (Viking Press, New York)

(The other half of the Snow Leopard story made famous by Matthiesson.)

Shresta, Singh and Pradham, *Ethnic Groups of Nepal and their Ways of Living* (HMG Press, Nepal)

The Story of the Mount Everest National Park (Cobb/Horwood Publishers, New Zealand)

(A lavishly illustrated book about the Khumbu written and edited by the park service. Full of good information.)

Snellgrove, David, *Himalayan Pilgrimage* (London, 1957)

Stainton, J.D.A., *Forests of Nepal* (Murray, London)

(Standard work on Nepal flora.)

Medical

Hackett, Peter, *Mountain Sickness: Prevention, Recognition and Treatment* (American Alpine Club, New York)

(Perhaps the best little booklet available, written by one of the most knowledgeable specialists.)

Houston, Charles, *Going High* (American Alpine Club)

Steele, Peter, *Medical Care for Mountain Climbers* (Heinemann, London)

Wilkerson, James A. *Medicine for Mountaineers* (The Mountaineers of Seattle)

(A comprehensive and practical book for doctors and laymen alike.)

For an up-to-date bibliography on all published articles and specific publications on mountain medicine, contact the UIAA Mountain Medicine Data Centre, c/o Dr Charles Clarke, St Bartholomew's Hospital, London.

Useful Addresses

ORGANISATIONS

The Alpine Club,
74 South Audley Street,
London W1Y 5FF
Tel: 01 499 1542
(Library open to the public)

Royal Geographical Society,
1 Kensington Gore,
London SW7 2AR
Tel: 01 589 5466
Runs Expedition Advisory Centre
Tel: 01 581 2057

British Mountaineering Council,
Crawford House,
Precinct Centre,
Booth Street East,
Manchester M13 9RZ
Tel: 061 146 0492

Himalayan Club,
PO Box 1905,
Bombay 400 001,
India

American Alpine Club,
113 East 90th Street,
New York, NY 10021
Tel: (212) 628 8383

American Adventurer's Association,
Suite 301,
444 NE Ravenna Blvd,
Seattle, WA 98115 USA
Tel: (206) 527 1621

Himalayan Rescue Association,
c/o Mountain Travel Nepal,
PO Box 170,
Kathmandu, Nepal

Sierra Club,
530 Bush Street,
San Francisco, CA 94108, USA

MAPS

Edward Stanford Ltd,
12–14 Long Acre,
Covent Garden,
London WC2E 9LP
Tel: 01 836 1321

The London Map Centre,
22–24 Caxton Street,
London SW1
Tel: 01 222 2466

The Map Centre Inc.,
2611 University Ave.,
San Diego,
CA 92104-2894, USA
Tel: (619) 291 3830

Library of Congress,
Geography and Map Division,
Washington DC 20540, USA

A worldwide listing in considerably more detail can be found in *The Travellers Handbook*, edited by Melissa Shales and published by WEXAS Ltd in the UK. In the USA an edition is put out by the Globe Pequot Press.

Index